Defense AGAINST Depression

THE WAY TO WHOLENESS

by Verdie Sather

AGLOW WORKSHOP SERIES

Women's Aglow Fellowship, Int'l.
P.O. Box I
Lynnwood, WA 98046-1558
USA

ATTENTION

Aglow workbooks have been published for the edification of every Christian and may be used by any individual group. However, unless a Bible study group is affiliated with Women's Aglow Fellowship, the name *Aglow* cannot be used in any way to designate the study group.

All references in this study are taken from the New American Standard Bible unless noted as follows: KJV (King James Version), JB (Jerusalem Bible), TLB (The Living Bible), TAB (The Amplified Bible), NIV (New International Version).

Cover design: Katherine VeHaun
Interior calligraphy: Janice Olson

Printed in the United States of America
Second printing 1984.
ISBN 0-930756-84-3

Write for free catalog.

Table of Contents

Introduction

Christians, as well as unbelievers, fall prey at times to depression in its various degrees. This emotional and physical illness is becoming a plague in God's Church, and few are those who have not at least tasted of it.

This Workbook is written for a two-fold audience: for those who are and want to remain victorious and strong in any trial they may experience; for others who find themselves either into a depression or teetering on the edge of it.

Through the past 22 years of helping my pastor-husband encourage saddened people, I have remained excited at seeing the permanent results that the Word of God and the power of the Holy Spirit can bring. Jesus Christ is not a crutch, as some would like to think, but an eternal refuge! Outside of Him, there is no guaranteed hope.

In his Epistle to the Corinthians, Paul wrote, *"We are...perplexed, but not despairing; persecuted, but not forsaken; struck down, but not destroyed" (2 Cor. 4:8,9)*. Even though there are times when circumstances almost plunge us into despair, there can be an undergirding of hope, comfort, and joy to the Spirit-filled child of God. This, then, is our ideal, and most of us are simply growing toward that goal.

There was a time in my own life, a time that lasted about a year, when I sincerely believed that I was beyond all hope. My testimony, however, is that the Lord "brought me...out of the miry clay, and set my feet upon a rock," and with His grace I am there to stay.

Verdie Sather

1

Biblical Examples

Starting Point

Solomon has written that there is nothing new under the sun. This is very true in the realm of human emotions. Great men and women of God have experienced deep feelings of sorrow and depression. Although the Word of God *does* have the answers to questions that trouble us at times, we sometimes fail to comprehend these answers for our needs.

Write down some of your own questions on this particular subject at the beginning of this study and later compare your ideas and questions with what you have learned.

The following paragraph brings out my knowledge of depressive feelings and the way I have been able to cope with them up until now.

I am taking this WORKSHOP for the following reasons:

I was reluctant to take this WORKSHOP because

In a few sentences describe the kind of fellowship you are enjoying with God at this time. If you have doubts about it, take this space to write your doubts.

Getting Acquainted

If you are in a group, at the beginning of your class, take a few minutes to introduce yourself and perhaps give a few facts concerning your family and its interests.

Group Discussion: How much of an effect do the circumstances of your life have on your spiritual joy? Are you happy because of, or in spite of, your lifestyle? Some of you may not be happy at all. Should every Christian be a happy person at all times?

The Lesson

Christians can expect trouble.

In the book of Job we read, *"For affliction does not come from the dust, neither does trouble sprout from the ground, for man is born for trouble, as sparks fly upward" (Job. 5:6,7).*

There is hope in the midst of trouble.

The most serious result of deep depression in individuals is the hopelessness that envelops them, a tactic of the enemy to destroy them. It should be greatly encouraging to know that many of the Bible writers were men who experienced emotional conflicts to the point of wanting to die. Yet, these were the very men who ultimately were used of God in the highest kind of inspiration; that of giving the world the Word of God.

There is purpose in the midst of trouble.

If God's purposes for these men brought great hope and usefulness, do you not believe that He has the same desires for His precious children today? The following passage of Scripture is worth meditating on for a few moments before you continue in this WORKSHOP, *"In this you greatly rejoice, even though now for a little while, if necessary, you have been distressed by various trials, that the proof of your faith, being more precious than gold which is perishable, even though tested by fire, may be found to result in praise and glory and honor at the revelation of Jesus Christ" (1 Pet. 1:6,7).*

What causes serious depressions?

Trouble itself is not a cause of depressions. They stem from human reactions and the way people view their troubles. We will be defining the various kinds of depressions in the next chapter and studying what God's Word has to say about them. In this chapter we will limit ourselves to the examples found in the Bible.

Who was our greatest example?

There is no doubt that Jesus had the greatest emotional conflicts of any human being because of the work He came to accomplish on our behalf. His conflicts were not His own but were the result of His identification with our sins. Jesus felt the complete result of our sins, which is death, and was tempted in all points just as we are.

Read Matthew 26:36-56.

1. How deeply did Jesus say He was grieved as a result of His coming death?_____

_____

2. What prayer did Jesus pray that shows us He had a problem facing the cross?_____

_____

3. How did Jesus' "friends" disappoint Him?_____

Read Luke 22:42-44.

4. What was the reaction of His great sorrow on His body?_____

_____

_____

Group Discussion: Would you like to share with your class an incident in your own life when a valued friend forsook you at a time of great need? How did you react, and how did it make you feel?

The effects of Jesus' anguish on His physical body.

The Holy Spirit uses the 69th Psalm as a prophecy, depicting in vivid detail Christ's coming death.

Read Psalm 69:1-3,7,20.

5. How did Jesus feel His suffering in the different parts of His body?

His feet _____

His throat _____

His eyes _____

His face _____

His heart _____

We see in this psalm how Jesus has taken the sinner's place. He felt the hopelessness of sinking in deep mire, a hopelessness that is akin to that of deep depression.

Read Luke 6:47,48.

6. Jesus took the results of our sins in identifying with us in our despair and hopelessness. What

kind of foundation has He provided for those who put their trust in Him?_____

_____

It is bad enough to feel forsaken by our valued friends, but it is worse to feel forsaken by our families or even by God!

7. How was Jesus feeling about His God and about His earthly family?

   Psalm 69:3; Matthew 27:46_____

   Psalm 69:8; John 7:5_____

_____

Most serious depressions begin with our reaction to various kinds of losses. Jesus *felt* the loss of friends for a time, the loss of family, and even the loss of the presence of His Father!
Read Matthew 27:11-14; Psalm 69:19.

8. In what ways did Jesus seemingly lose His reputation?_____

_____

Group Discussion: Can you discuss other ways in which Jesus felt extremely alone at this time?

9. What does the following scripture tell us about another kind of loss that Jesus felt in order to identify with us?

   2 Corinthians 8:9 _____

   _____

Exercise 1   Take a few minutes with your class at this time to admit to the Lord that you know He truly understands you and cares about you and your needs. In the days ahead speak aloud your praise for all that He wants to be to you.

Exercise 2   If, through your trust in the Lord, you have ever had a victory over a financial loss, would you share it with your classmates?

Jesus overcame His temptation to despair.
Read Matthew 14:23; Mark 1:35.
10. Jesus had great temptation to despair. How did He overcome it?

_____

11. What was His admonition to the disciples after they had fallen asleep in the garden?

_____

Read 1 Peter 5:8.

12. What reason is given in this passage of scripture for being alert and watchful?

_____

_____

Satan is always alert to make use of every opportunity to bring all people to a point of discouragement and hopelessness, so he can destroy them. This is his main purpose for every individual. He is working overtime these days to sadden God's children.

Group Discussion: Is it possible for Christians to be aware of many of Satan's tactics and yet remain mentally healthy and positive in their outlook over their circumstances? When our armies go to war, we want them to be positive and trusting for victory at the same time that we give them knowledge concerning the enemy.

Overwhelming burdens are felt by Moses.

Read Numbers 11:1-4, 10-15.

Moses was beginning to feel a loss of confidence in his leadership over the people of Israel. Perhaps the people's confidence in his ability was also at stake. The complaints of the people concerning their lack of food had angered the Lord, and Moses was also displeased. Resentment and anger sometimes arise as a result of a loss in people's lives.

13. After reading the prayer Moses offered to God, write down in your own words how Moses was

feeling about himself._____

_____

_____

_____

14. How was he feeling about the Lord? Put this down in your own words also._____

_____

15. What did Moses ask the Lord to do at the end of his prayer?_____

_____

_____

There are three things that seem to go together: anger as a result of a loss, self-pity, and depression.

Read Numbers 11:16,17.

Group Discussion: How do you view God's response to Moses' anger against Him? Why didn't God remonstrate with Moses concerning his lack of faith?

Exercise 3   You may never have had the responsibility of a man like Moses, but perhaps in a small way you have felt a load too heavy to bear. Write down your progression from a loss, to anger, and then depression. Try to remember how long it lasted. Would you like to share this with your class?

Exercise 4   Now take a little time to thank the Lord for understanding and giving you the victory! If you're in a depression at the present time, it is good to give Him thanks for what He is *going* to do for you.

Read Numbers 11:11,12; 1 Peter 5:7; Psalm 55:22.

Discussion Question: In the light of the above scriptures, write down what you see as a weakness in the faith of Moses.

Elijah was tormented by fear and a desire to die.
Read 1 Kings 19:1-10.

Elijah had performed a great miracle through the power of God and had shown the people who was the truly great God in comparison to an idol, Baal. Then, Queen Jezebel threatened his life and Elijah ran.

16. What did Elijah request of the Lord in verse 4?_____

Have you noticed how God ministered to Elijah in spite of his fear and depression? What a merciful God we have!

17. How was Elijah's loneliness revealed in verse 10?_____

_____

Group Discussion: Can you think of other ways Elijah was depressed?

Read 1 Kings 19:10; Deuteronomy 31:6.
18. In the light of the above scriptures, what was the weakness in Elijah's faith?_____

_____

Jeremiah shared God's anguish over Israel.
Read Jeremiah 9:1,2; 10:19,20; 15:10,18.

Jeremiah's message was not only a sorrow to Israel, but to Jeremiah as well. He appeared as a traitor to his countrymen by prophesying submission to a strange country and king. Yet, this was God's message! (Jer. 27:6-15).

19. Jeremiah's depression and sorrow were very descriptive! Can you describe them in your own

words?_____

_____

_____

Read Jeremiah 15:16,20,21.

20. How did Jeremiah get strength to endure this pain, and what did God promise him?_____

_____

_____

Read Jeremiah 15:10; Hebrews 12:2,3; Nehemiah 8:10.

21. In the light of the above scriptures, what was the temporary weakness in this man's faith?

_____

_____

Group Discussion: At the very beginning of this lesson, you were asked the question, What effect do your circumstances have on your happiness? Can you differentiate between what the world calls happiness and what the Christian calls joy?

Group Discussion: Can there be joy at a time when we are going through a heavy trial?

Exercise 5 One of the ways we can have our joy restored is to take a few minutes just to praise and worship God for His promised inheritance to us. Jesus looked forward to His inheritance, and we are admonished to do the same. Let's do it right now!

Jonah was full of rebellion.
Read Jonah 4:1-11.

Jonah was a prophet of God sent to preach to the great city of Nineveh. He was slow to obey, and God had to deal strongly with him. Some of these great prophets of the Bible had the same traits we see manifested in Christians today, and yet God used them mightily. What an encouragement to us!

Group Discussion: What do you think was the underlying cause of Jonah's rebellion and ultimate depression?

22. How was Jonah's anger and self-pity manifested?_____

_____

23. How did God show His mercy toward Jonah in spite of his anger?_____

_____

Group Discussion: What are some of the prejudices that people have today that could result in depression?

Read Jonah 3:4,5,10; 4:1,9-11; Luke 15:10; 2 Peter 3:9.

24. In the light of the above scriptures, what were Jonah's spiritual weaknesses?_____

_____

Continue at Home

To search yourself

1. Am I going to continue to remind myself to look to Jesus as my example in every emotional conflict? Do I really believe that He understands and can instill hope in me?

2. Am I going to prepare myself for future problems or even a trauma by continued obedience to the Word of God?

3. Can I begin to make a practice of being alert and watchful for any attack of the enemy that could throw me into despair?

4. How can I learn to take one day at a time and trust the Lord to give me grace and strength for that day alone? (Matt. 6:34).

To do

1. Search your Bible for other examples of men or women who have had a serious problem of discouragement and have found victory in the Lord.

2. Make a practice each morning in your devotions to ask the Lord to remind you to cast each care and tendency to worry on Him. Prepare to *leave* them all there and depend on the Lord for strength to cope.

3. Be sure to have that time alone with the Lord each day without fail. To help you with this, see Diary Entry page at the end of this chapter.

To focus

What has been the most encouraging and outstanding thought of this chapter to me?

How will I use this to help me be a blessing to someone else this week?

To memorize

"Casting all your anxiety upon Him, because He cares for you" (1 Pet. 5:7).

"Keep watching and praying, that you may not enter into temptation; the spirit is willing, but the flesh is weak" (Matt. 26:41).

"I will rejoice and be glad in Thy lovingkindness, because Thou hast seen my affliction; Thou hast known the troubles of my soul, and Thou hast not given me over into the hand of the enemy" (Ps. 31:7).

Diary Entry

   At the end of each chapter is a diary entry page. Spend some time each day with the Lord. Record the time spent in prayer and what the Lord shows you.

DIARY ENTRY

DAY	TIME SPENT WITH THE LORD	SPECIAL TRUTHS THE LORD SHOWED ME

Monday

Tuesday

Wednesday

Thursday

Friday

Saturday

2

Sorrowful Emotions

Starting Point

In our studies from Lesson One, I was greatly encouraged in the following ways:

I believe that the following suggestions could make my days more worthwhile and interesting: (Time for the following would be approximate.)

Fellowshiping with the Lord in worship and devotion_____

Exercising _____

Sharing with a friend over the phone_____

Time out for an interesting hobby_____

A good walk in the fresh air_____

Playing with my children_____

Getting Acquainted

At the beginning of your class today, discuss with your neighbor your favorite hobby if you have one.

Group Discussion: Share briefly with one another any progress you have made in adjusting to daily problems as a result of Lesson One. Has any close family member noticed the difference in you? How did she/he react?

The Lesson

All sorrow is a result of man's fall into sin.

Every kind of sorrow that you could name, whether constructive or destructive, was never God's intention for His human creation. He made all things beautiful for Adam and Eve: the garden with its plentiful fruits and beauty, and His Presence to give fellowship and glory.

Through Christ's redemptive death on the cross, God is in the process of restoring us to His original purpose.

Read Isaiah 35:10; Revelation 21:3,4.

1. What kind of joy will be on the heads of God's people? _____

2. From the two passages above, make a list of the negative things that will someday pass away

forever. _____

_____

In the meantime, because of sin, man is born into a world of trouble.

Read John 16:33.

3. Why is it possible for the Christian to be of good cheer in the midst of tribulation?

_____

God uses sorrow in a constructive way.

4. Write out in your own words the following passage of scripture.

2 Corinthians 7:9-11_____

_____

_____

_____

The scripture shows that sorrow for sin is not enough, but that it can lead us to repentance, which is important for every person. It means that we actually turn our lives over to Jesus. It means turning from going our own way and going God's way.

Read Luke 14:33 with Acts 11:26.

5. What kind of people were first called Christians?_____

Group Discussion: What does it mean to be a disciple of Jesus?

Read 2 Corinthians 7:10 again.

6. What does this passage have to say about the sorrow of the world?_____

Group Discussion: What was the difference in the kind of sorrow Peter manifested after he had denied Jesus, and the kind of sorrow Judas Iscariot felt following his betrayal of Jesus? (Luke 22:61,62; Matt. 27:3-5).

Group Discussion: If we know that we have been forgiven by the Lord for our past sins, how can we keep from being remorseful about them?

Exercise 1   Bow your heads for three minutes. Even though you have asked God for forgiveness, ask yourself if you are still remorseful over your past life.

Exercise 2   If you have truly accepted God's forgiveness for yourself, spend another three minutes praising the Lord for the liberty you are enjoying. If you are still unhappy and suffering guilt, ask God to free you to really believe that you are forgiven. Be sure to ask God to forgive you; then accept your release from all self-condemnation.

Read 2 Corinthians 6:10.

Group Discussion: In what ways can a Christian be sorrowful and yet rejoice?

Read Psalm 126:5,6.
7. If we sow in tears, how will we reap?_____

Personal Question: Have you ever felt genuine sorrow for the state of those who are lost? Ask the Lord to give you a little part in feeling the way He feels about them.

Read Romans 9:1-3.
8. How did Paul feel about his kinsmen, the Israelites?_____

_____

_____

   If we will enter into the kind of sorrow that God wants us to feel for those around us, we will begin to get a better perspective of our own circumstances.

Mourning the loss of a loved one is a normal sorrow.
   God can use this kind of sorrow in a constructive way, also. When individuals are set aside for a time of grieving, it can help them to reevaluate their life and put their perspectives in good order. It can strengthen their relationship with the Lord and His other children.

Group Discussion: Can you think of various ways your life was made stronger after the loss of a close friend or family member?

Group Discussion: Some of you may have had very severe difficulties to face. Would you care to relate these to your classmates? If someone is still in deep sorrow, a few minutes of prayer would be wise at this point.

Jesus never leaves us without hope!
Read John 16:19-22.

9. What did Jesus expect the disciples to do after He left them?_____

_____

10. What was the hope He gave them?_____

_____

Read Isaiah 61:1-3.

11. What does the Lord promise to do for the following:

The afflicted?_____

The brokenhearted?_____

The captives?_____

The mourners in Zion?_____

_____

Read Luke 4:17-21.

12. *When* were these scriptures in Isaiah fulfilled?_____

_____

Normal sorrow can accompany trials and persecution.
Read 2 Corinthians 1:3-8.

13. Paul sometimes despaired of his own life in the trials he went through. How did he write about

the comfort the Lord Jesus gives?_____

_____

_____

14. Look up the various meanings for the word *depression* in the dictionary._____

_____

Group Discussion: Discuss these various meanings with your class. Can you decide which definition is really the best?

Depression initially means "to press down."

Depression is rightly named because the results of sin on mankind have been to press down on the bubbling joy and happiness that God intended for us in the first place. As we have already seen, this shall be restored!

Group Discussion: We have already mentioned the loss of loved ones as a cause of sorrow. Depression can begin in our life by our reaction to this loss. Can you name some other losses in our life that could be the beginning of a serious depression?

Group Discussion: Should we ever try to stop anyone from having a normal period of time for grieving?

Read John 11:32-38.

15. This passage is only a part of the story of Lazarus, whom Jesus raised from the dead. How did

Jesus relate to the grieving of his friends, Mary and Martha?_____

_____

Read 1 Corinthians 15:53-57.

16. Fill in the blanks of the following scripture. *"This perishable must put on the imperishable, and*

this mortal must put on immortality. But _____ this perishable will have put on the im-

perishable, and this mortal will have put on immortality, _____ _____ _____

_____ _____ _____, that is written, 'Death is swallowed up in victory.'"

17. According to the above verse, when will death cease to be an enemy to the Christian?_____

_____

Group Discussion: We know that for the true Christian, death has lost its sting. However, death is still an enemy in several ways. What are they?

Grieving is a necessary experience.

Sometimes the shock a person goes through in losing a loved one causes her to deny that the death has actually taken place. When the truth is made clear, the next step is to try to blame someone. Perhaps resentment arises against God or even oneself. Under normal conditions of bereavement, this phase soon passes and a real time of grieving sets in. This is very necessary for the health of the individual, and, after a certain amount of time, the grieving is resolved. In the next lessons, we will be considering what can transpire if bitterness, anger and self-pity are allowed to continue.

Sorrow is a normal reaction to the losses we face in life.

If we are to remain healthy, both spiritually and physically, sorrow must be resolved after a normal time of grieving. Our spiritual health will depend on how we view our loss and how we allow our confidence in the Lord to grow. Our physical health may also be dependent upon that.

Holding on to our sorrow in a lingering sadness can cause a state of depression that will be detrimental to our whole being. We can control quite well what goes into our conscious mind, but it is our subconscious mind that affects the glands of our body. This part of us takes its food from the conscious part of our brain, and, if that food is negative thinking, sickness can be the result. Depression then takes control of the person.

God tests our commitment to Him.

The more materialistic we are, the more we are apt to experience deep depression over loss of *things,* such as jobs, possessions, etc.

Read 1 Timothy 6:6-11.

18. What does the Bible tell us about the way we came into this world, and the way we go out?

_____

19. What should we be content with?_____

> **Exercise 3**   It might be a good idea to look up the word *contentment* in a dic-
> tionary and see the various meanings. The Greek word, *Arkeo,* em-
> bodies the idea of letting food and raiment be sufficient to satisfy us.

Practice commitment daily.

If, as a daily habit, we can learn to hold our possessions "lightly" and look at them as very tem-
poral, then, when a day of loss comes, we will not be so "torn apart."

We have God's promise to take care of us.

Sometimes God allows losses in our life in order for us to see a little clearer where our priorities
are. If we have a stronger attachment to anyone or anything than to the Lord, we could be setting
ourself up for a deep depression in the future. Sometimes we are not aware of this until we experience
the loss.

20. What does this same scripture in Timothy tell us about those who want to get rich?

_____

_____

Group Discussion: Does this mean that God doesn't want anyone to have a large amount of money
or possessions?

Read 1 Timothy 6:17-19; Philippians 4:11-13, 19.

21. In these scriptures we read the instructions God gives to those who are rich. Write these down

in your own words._____

_____

_____

Group Discussion: We know that it is God's will for His children to prosper. From your study so
far, how do you think the Bible evaluates that prosperity? Would you say that it is prosperity for
God to supply our needs?

22. What was Paul's attitude toward whatever state he found himself in?_____

Personal Question: Do you feel that you can identify with Paul in his attitude, or are you having a
real difficulty with it?

The Apostle Paul is our example.

At times most of us lack complete trust in the Lord's promise to help us through our losses, but we
want to press into the kind of attitude Paul had when he wrote that he had learned "to be content in
whatsoever state I am." As we grow in our Christian experience, we also grow in faith.

Group Discussion: All people have a reaction to loss. What do you think is the difference between
a healthy grief and the beginnings of an unhealthy depression? We have already looked at some of
this.

Depression can be a habit.

Many children are growing up in families with very depressive lifestyles. Divorce and child abuse are prevalent in our society today. If this situation continues, it causes changes in the victims' physical condition and perpetuates depression. This situation is not hopeless because we serve a God of miracles, but in the natural it takes medication and careful counseling. In our studies we will limit ourselves to the kind of depression that results from our reaction to losses of various kinds.

 # Continue at Home

To search yourself

1. How can I make the promises of God applicable to my everyday experiences?

2. Do I have a natural tendency to look at the negative or the positive side of circumstances? What does the Lord want me to do about the situation?

3. Have I been able to enter into the kind of sorrow that the Lord has for those outside of His protective care so that I can pray effectively for them?

To do

1. From time to time, we all need to ask God for forgiveness. This is why Jesus functions today as our High Priest. When we ask for forgiveness, we need to remember that repentance must accompany it. If, as far as we understand, we are truly repenting, we can avoid much self-condemnation.

2. If you have not established a habit of meeting with the Lord each day, be sure that this becomes a daily practice. It should become the "highlight" of each day!

3. Make a habit of speaking only good of those you talk about.

To focus

The idea that stands out in this lesson is

I can use it this week by

To memorize

"These things I have spoken to you, that in Me you may have peace. In the world you have tribulation, but take courage; I have overcome the world" (John 16:33).

"Peace I leave with you; My peace I give to you; not as the world gives, do I give to you. Let not your heart be troubled, not let it be fearful" (John 14:27).

"When I am afraid, I will put my trust in Thee. In God, whose Word I praise, in God I have put my trust; I shall not be afraid. What can mere man do to me?" (Ps. 56:3,4).

DIARY ENTRY

DAY	TIME SPENT WITH THE LORD	SPECIAL TRUTHS THE LORD SHOWED ME

Monday

Tuesday

Wednesday

Thursday

Friday

Saturday

3

Results of Continual Anger

Starting Point

In grieving over a particular loss in my life, I can identify the following steps that lead into a depression:

I have a tendency to become angry when:

I get over my anger: In a few minutes_____. In a day or two_____. Sometimes I

hold a grudge_____.

All through this Bible study, we want to look at the subjects under discussion from the viewpoint of a Christian who sincerely wants to serve and obey the Lord. We definitely want to study what Scripture has to say about these things and to apply its truth to the trials we go through. God's *hope* is the only real *hope!*

Our enemy is out to destroy the works of God and especially His human creation. When we become angry, we cooperate with Satan, and anger, carried to excess, can result in serious symptoms that in turn lead to disaster.

In our next chapter we will show from Scripture that anger can be a normal human reaction. Under certain conditions, it may not be sinful. There were times when God was very angry, and we will see how very angry Jesus became over the loss of respect for His Father's house! However, in this lesson, we will study the consequences of continued and hurtful anger.

Getting Acquainted

Take a partner from your group and share together one of the first things you remember in your childhood, and how it affected you.

Group Discussion: It might be a good idea for those of you who have been filled with the Holy Spirit to share with the others how this experience has affected your ability to cope with anger.

The Lesson

God's Word warns us of the dangers of continued anger.

1. Rewrite the following verses in your own words.

Proverbs 29:22_____

_____

Proverbs 14:17_____

_____

Ecclesiastes 7:9_____

_____

I shall never forget a very depressed and angry man who once stayed with us while we endeavored to lead him to the Lord. A truck driver had run over and killed his wife and two children many years before. Because he was not willing to forgive that truck driver, he could not accept forgiveness from the Lord Jesus for himself. How we pleaded with him! One night he left our home. We lost contact with this man, but later he hitchhiked a ride with a man, took his credentials, and killed him, leaving him on the side of the road. Long after, this man was found, tried for murder and given the electric chair. Even though he had only been angry at the truck driver, his grudge caused him to murder an innocent man. His reaction to the loss of his family now cost him his own life!

Read Psalm 55:3b.

2. What does the last part of this verse tell us about anger?_____

Read Hebrews 12:15.

3. What can be the result if we continue to hold resentment in our hearts?_____

_____

Group Discussion: Can you name some ways that many people can be hurt by this attitude?

The "hard to get along with" person needs our love.

Many times, we come across people who are actually soured on life in general. Something has happened to these people. They may have been raised in an atmosphere where love is a scarcity and punishment abounds. They need a caring group of Christians who will give them the warmth and love that they lack, Christians who will listen and share with them from the very depth of their own hearts. Some people are depressed because of their own nature.

Read Proverbs 19:19.

4. If someone delivers this kind of a person out of a mess, what will be the result?_____

_____

A person who has an irritable and angry disposition will get herself into many difficulties. Thank God for the miracle He wants to do for such people. What so many discouraged people fail to understand is that depression is a choice we make. We can choose to be happy or to be sad. We can choose to hang on to our resentful anger, or to let it be resolved through proper channels. Satan has succeeded in making many think that depression has come on through the circumstances they find themselves in. This is untrue! Rather, it is their reaction to these circumstances. We can choose to obey the Word of God or to disregard it. We can choose to be good to ourselves or to punish ourselves. What is your choice?

While anger is a natural defense against our losses of family, jobs, health, insult, rejection, or even reputation, it can be destructive. When we choose to indulge in anger or hold grudges, Satan uses it to destroy us physically, emotionally, and spiritually.

Anger can be physically destructive.

Read 1 Corinthians 6:19,20; 3:16,17.

5. Continued anger can destroy us physically. When we are truly God's child, who is the sole

possessor of our bodies?_____

6. What are we, therefore, commanded to do with our bodies?_____

_____

Group Discussion: Since we are bought with a price, what are some of the ways we must glorify God with our bodies?

7. What does the Lord tell us about those who destroy the temple of God?_____

_____

Exercise 1   Bow your head right now and think back to a time when you
                   were very angry. Can you recall how this affected you
                   physically? Now for a few minutes, share with your class how
                   you felt.

Nothing produces stress as much as anger, and our body can stand only so much of this.
Many times anger is the direct cause of ulcers, headaches, high blood pressure, colitis and
many other physical ailments. Some people have dropped dead during an angry outburst.
Anger doesn't only need to be controlled, but also resolved. This will be dealt with in our
next lesson.

When people first become resentful over some loss, they frequently vent their anger on
the one who has hurt them. Then as time goes on they can begin to resent and blame
themselves for their part in the situation. This self-condemnation, if continued, can lead to
suicidal tendencies. This is exactly what the enemy wants: the destruction of the body!

Read 1 Thessalonians 5:22,23.

8. What is Paul's prayer for the bodies of God's dear people?_____

_____

_____

Read 1 Corinthians 7:2-5.

9. Continued resentment toward our husband can cause sexual frigidity. What is the Scrip-

tural injunction given to wives in this passage_____

_____

_____

Depriving a husband of his sexual fulfillment can be a form of inverted punishment or
revenge on him. Yet if anger has made us sexually frigid, we think we can justify ourself.
The only thing that can make a difference is a change of attitude. We must view our husband as God views him. A woman who had resented her husband for many years went to
a doctor about her sexual frigidity but received no help. Finally, she left her husband and
ran into the arms of another man where she found she wasn't as frigid as she had thought.
What a way to find out! She had nursed grudges and had been in a state of depression all
her married life. Sexual frigidity, then, can be a bodily reaction to resentment.

The emotional reactions to anger and bitterness can be devastating.
Read Romans 3:10,14; Ephesians 4:30-32.

10. The non-Christian can be full of bitterness. The Christian should deal with it immediately.

Look up this word *bitter* in a dictionary and write what you find._____

_____

You can only take so much of this kind of stress without becoming distraught.
Remember the man who nursed his grudge against the truck driver who had killed his
family and who eventually killed an innocent man.

Anger causes even greater spiritual damage.

Saul, through disobedience, lost his fellowship with God and Samuel. If he had truly repented, he could have been forgiven. However, his loss turned to jealousy and anger against David.

Read 1 Samuel 15:34,35; 16:1.

11. How much was involved in the loss that Saul suffered?_____

_____

Read 1 Samuel 20:30,31.

12. What was Saul now planning to do to David?_____

Read Psalm 55:1-3,12,13.

13. Why was it so hard for David to bear the sorrow of Saul's anger and grudge?_____

_____

Read 1 Chronicles 10:13,14.

14. What else did Saul do because of his emotional and spiritual loss?_____

_____

15. The history of the life of King Saul is a sad commentary on the spiritual result of anger and

bitterness. What was the end result?_____

Group Discussion: Why does it seem so impossible for some Christians to get their help from the Word of God and the power of the Holy Spirit today?

The purpose of this lesson is to show some of the results of continuing in anger and resentment. The Lord wants His children to have real victory no matter what our circumstances are and no matter what others may do to us.

Results of anger grieve the Holy Spirit.

Read Ephesians 4:30-32.

16. While we are putting away our anger and resentment, what should be our positive reaction?

_____

_____

Group Discussion: We have the potential and capacity to be kind and tenderhearted instead of angry. After we have invited God's Spirit to take control, how can we begin to do this? Take 1 Corinthians 13:5,6 into consideration as you answer this question.

These are some thoughts that will lead us into our next lesson.

Exercise 2   Divide the class into groups of four and discuss, if you can remember, a time of anger and the loss that caused it. If there was victory, take a little time to praise the Lord; for those who are still hurting, take some time to pray.

Now spend some time together to seek the Lord for His enlightenment on Lesson Three, asking Him for power to put it into practice in your life.

Continue at Home

To search yourself

1. The Holy Spirit has shown me the following areas in my own life where resentment is still taking a toll over my joy in the Lord:_____

_____

_____

2. Can I honestly say that at this moment I have only good feelings toward everyone that I know? If not, can I trust the Lord to show me a proper procedure to resolve the bad feelings?

To do

1. Whether I am defeated by anger and resentment or whether I am victorious, I shall proceed to look for positive characteristics in all those I have anything to do with. This fulfills 1 Corinthians 13:5,6.

2. I can and will, with the power given me through the Holy Spirit, take care of my physical body as the temple in which *He* dwells.

3. Fill in the following lines if they apply to a situation in your life. In my resentment I suffered in the following ways:

Physically _____

Mentally_____

Spiritually _____

To focus

The idea that stands out to me in this lesson is

I can use it this week by

To memorize

"Or do you not know that your body is a temple of the Holy Spirit who is in you, whom you have from God, and that you are not your own? For you have been bought with a price: therefore glorify God in your body" (1 Cor. 6:19,20).

"And do not grieve the Holy Spirit of God, by whom you were sealed for the day of redemption. Let all bitterness and wrath and anger and clamor and slander be put away from you" (Eph. 4:30,31).

Diary Entry

Continue to record the time you spend each day reading God's Word and praying. Also record what the Lord shows you that gives you joy.

DIARY ENTRY

DAY	TIME SPENT WITH THE LORD	SPECIAL TRUTHS THE LORD SHOWED ME

Monday

Tuesday

Wednesday

Thursday

Friday

Saturday

4

Resolving My Anger

Starting Point

As a result of our study in Lesson Three, I am learning to face my problems by

I am beginning to learn that I have weaknesses in the following areas of my character:

I am a sorrowful person: All of the time _____
                          Most of the time _____
                          Once in a while _____
                          Seldom, if ever_____

The following paragraph explains why I feel this way.

Anger is a normal emotion and is not necessarily a sinful thing. Using a concordance, can you find some scriptures that show God as being angry at times? You may also find some scriptures where Jesus became very angry. List them below.

Getting Acquainted

Take a partner from your group and relate to her an incident in your life that made you extremely happy.

Group Discussion: What do you think is the difference between anger and hostility? Perhaps later you can look up the meanings in the dictionary.

The Lesson

Anger can be a first step into a serious depression.

When we add our own reactions, such as anger and resentment, to a normal grief, we are in trouble. Most depressions begin with resentment of some kind. We understand from the Bible that anger in itself is not a sin, but the real problem comes in the way we resolve that anger. I am convinced that good, sound scriptural teaching and sound mental health go together. I am also convinced that the only true and complete answer to life's problems is found in the Word of God.

The non-Christian and the Christian face many of the same conflicts today, but the Christian has resources to fall back on that the non-Christian doesn't have. There is no lasting hope outside of our wonderful Jesus.

We must grasp solid scriptural truths.

The loss of one important person, whether by death or by divorce, can result in a reaction of anger. This can be short-lived or lasting, depending on how we grasp God's Truth. We have a deep need to be loved.

Read 1 John 4:9,10; John 3:16; Romans 5:6-8, 10; Ephesians 2:8,9; Jeremiah 31:3.

1. God's love was made known to us through the Word of God. What do the above passages tell you about God's love for us:

Who is included? _____

What He did to show that love? _____

_____

When He loved us? _____

What kind of love He had for us?_____

Our condition when He loved us? _____

_____

Read Ephesians 1:5-8.
2. Write down some of the things that were included when God so graciously accepted us?

_____

_____

God is the most important of persons! Being accepted by Him and realizing that He so desires a close family tie with us that He was willing to die to accomplish this, needs to be thoroughly grasped. The only way this can be grasped is by believing what God's Word says.
Read John 1:12,13.
3. Who are the ones that God gives power to become His children?_____

_____

When we receive Him, God gives us a measure of faith by which we are truly born-again into the family of God. This can be the beginning of *hope* in the midst of despair, based on the reality of the Word.

Exercise 1   Once more name some losses as examples and show how resentment can begin.

The non-Christian, when faced with a significant loss, usually sees God not as His Father, but rather as a moralist who is now facing him with His truth. The Christian who has a firm grasp on Bible knowledge sees God as a Father who has mixed His Truth with deep love, grace and mercy. This can eventually be a source of comfort to bring him through his crisis.

However, because so many Christians find themselves deeply frustrated, and possibly even in shock at times, we need to be often reminded gently of the reality of God's presence and Word.

Group Discussion: In your estimation, are the following statements true or false? "If I am a Christian, I should never get angry." "If I do get angry, I must not express it." "I must express my anger very vehemently if necessary to let others know how angry I am." If this last statement is true, how would we affect those upon whom we vented our anger?

Anger may be properly dealt with.
Read Ephesians 4:26,27,31.
4. This scripture brings out the fact that we should allow anger, but what is the command that

follows it? _____

_____

_____

Exercise 2   Write a paragraph on the difference between being human and being sinful. How can you be angry and feel emotion without sinning?

Group Discussion: Now share some of your written ideas with your class for discussion.

Read John 2:13-17; Psalm 69:9.

5. How did Jesus express His anger when He came into the Temple?_____

_____

_____

6. What kind of zeal caused this expression?_____

_____

Group Discussion: What kind of a threat did Jesus sense in the attitudes of the people toward His Father's house?

To protect oneself or one's possessions is a very human trait and God has instilled this in us for a very good reason. It is part of the self-preservation instinct. When this is threatened in any way, anger and resentment are aroused. This in turn causes a deep emotional feeling.

We can be sure that Jesus was in complete control of His anger, even though He expressed it in "no uncertain terms." It is not wrong for Christians to express anger at what Satan does in the lives of people, or at what sin does in them. Jesus certainly did not continue in His anger, since later He died for these same people.

Read Luke 23:34.

7. What was Jesus' prayer to His Father concerning these men while hanging on the cross?

_____

When we try to make ourselves less than human by denying our anger, or failing to express it, we can eventually hurt ourselves. We must learn to express it without hostility.

Read 1 Peter 4:1; 1:6,7; 4:12,13.

Accepting the fact that we will experience some losses during our lifetime can help us to cope with them when they come. Thus, we will become less angry and we will be more able to express our anger in a constructive way.

8. Fill in the last part of the following Scripture. *"Therefore, since Christ has suffered in the flesh,*

_____

_____

Group Discussion: It would be helpful at this time to discuss together what you think is the meaning of the last half of this verse of scripture.

9. God has a purpose for the losses that we face in life. There are some purposes listed in the above

scripture. See if you can find them and write them down._____

_____

If we learn to know God's Word and recognize His leading in every event we encounter, our confidence will increase and our fears lessen. A Christian psychiatrist once told us that behind every angry outburst is a deep-seated fear of some kind. God wants to lessen these fears by instilling His Word into our hearts. Learning to trust our God lessens fear! Recognition that we live in an imperfect world helps us face the fact that we will have losses and threats of losses. This recognition will help us cope with whatever circumstances we find ourselves in without too much fear. Therefore, we will have less anger.

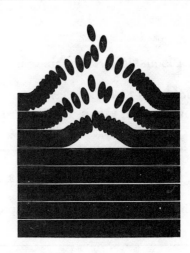

Read Psalm 37:8, Colossians 3:8.

10. What does Scripture command us to do about our anger?_____

_____

The sin can be in the continuation of these feelings within us. We hurt ourselves and cause bitterness to take root in our hearts. Eventually, we can hurt others as well.

Read Romans 12:19.

11. Why can we afford to lay aside our anger and wrath?_____

_____

God is fair, and He can see the hearts of all people. He knows how to repay them for what they have done. He is also willing to forgive.

Personal Question: Are you willing to forgive those who have made you angry?

The Bible has the only answer for angry and depressed people. It has the power to build faith and confidence in our God. Believing what God says about His ability to avenge us in all things will relieve us of much of our anger. At least, it can put us in control of our emotions.

Group Discussion: If anger itself is not a sin, when can it become a sin for us?

12. How do you see the following verses?

Proverbs 15:8_____

_____

Proverbs 16:32_____

_____

Read Joel 2:13.

13. What great example do we have?_____

Read Colossians 3:8.

14. What are we commanded to lay aside?_____

From the above scriptures, we see that uncontrolled anger, in the form of a quick temper, and temper that goes on and on without being resolved, can and *will* bring on depression and guilt. The important questions we face are how do we resolve our anger and how do we cease from it? Here are some ways.

Read 3 John 1:4.

15. How are to to walk?_____

We need to accept the fact that we are angry and "own up" to it.

Read James 5:16.

16. If our anger has been one of continued bitterness, what are we to do?_____

If God knows how to take vengeance, shouldn't we be willing to give up our desire to get even with those who have hurt us? This should be the next step.

Read Matthew 5:23,24; 18:15-17.

17. We see a good way to express our anger constructively and with good control in these scriptures.

Put this down in your own words._____

_____

_____

_____

This should be done as soon as it is possible, and not put off. Ephesians 4:26 instructs us not to let the sun go down on our wrath. Sometimes we cannot reach the other person until later, but we can make up our mind to take care of it as soon as possible. In the meantime, let's make it right with the Lord and refuse to be wrathful about it.

A friend had done me an injustice, and I became very angry. A phone call took care of it. In firm but controlled words, I expressed exactly how I felt about the situation and she apologized. It lifted a big load, and we were friends once more. If I had lost my temper with her, she might have retaliated in kind, and amplified the problem between us. So many times we are afraid to face the offender. We would rather suffer untold misery! It is a command from the Lord to take care of these situations.

If I had retaliated with my friend in kind, I would have only added guilt to my anger. Since Christ in me gave me the strength, I could obey Jesus in not avenging myself. This way I found myself free to take care of the problem with her.

Group Discussion: What are some of the ways that we can face an offender and resolve our anger?

We do not need to come in an accusatory manner, but rather ask the person if she really meant to do what she did? Perhaps you misunderstood the person. Perhaps you can tell that person something that you like about her first, and then present her with the problem. The Holy Spirit is the very best judge of human nature and if we need wisdom for the occasion, He will give it to us.

Read Matthew 18:21-35; James 2:10.

18. Write a paragraph after reading the above passages, and show the reasons why we should be

quick to forgive others who sin against us. _____

_____

_____

_____

Group Discussion: Can you think of some ways a person can express her anger if the offender has died, or cannot be reached?

Sometimes we can go to our pastor or someone we have confidence in and tell him about our deep bitterness in this regard. After prayer together, and knowing that God has forgiven us, we should be able to resolve that anger and lay it aside.

 # Continue at Home

To search yourself

1. If you are resentful toward someone at this moment, what is the cause? Have you cut off communication with her?

2. If you are a divorced woman, are you still harboring resentment toward your former spouse?

3. Perhaps you have not recognized your anger. Do you find yourself being extremely critical or argumentative with those who are close to you?

4. If any of these questions "hit home" with you, try to take care of the problem according to the pattern laid down in God's Word. Waiting upon God in earnest prayer will give you wisdom as to how to respond.

To do

If you are depressed, then you are possibly angry about something in your circumstances. Try to look at yourself by filling in the following lines.

Subject of loss or fear of loss_____

I became resentful of _____

_____

I took out my anger on _____

_____

My depression has lasted_____

_____

This has affected my spiritual life in the following ways: _____

_____

_____

The Lord is helping me by_____

_____

To focus

The idea that stands out to me in this lesson is

I can use it this week by

To memorize

"Be angry, and yet do not sin; do not let the sun go down on your anger, and do not give the devil an opportunity" (Eph. 4:26,27).

"And be kind to one another, tender-hearted, forgiving each other, just as God in Christ also has forgiven you" (Eph. 4:32).

Diary Entry

Waiting on the Lord in reading His Word and prayer time is vital for a happy and undepressed spirit. Record each day's time for this on your diary page.

DIARY ENTRY

DAY	TIME SPENT WITH THE LORD	SPECIAL TRUTHS THE LORD SHOWED ME
Monday		
Tuesday		
Wednesday		
Thursday		
Friday		
Saturday		

5

"Ye Fearful Saints, Fresh Courage Take."

Starting Point

I am learning to resolve my anger as a result of Lesson Four in the following way:

In the coming week I am going to look at as many scriptures as I can find in the concordance on the subject of anger and record what I find each day.

Sunday _____

Monday _____

Tuesday _____

Wednesday _____

Thursday _____

Friday _____

Saturday _____

Jesus said to the disciples, *"Why are you timid, you men of little faith?"* How true it is, that timidity and fear are the opposites of real faith! As we proceed in this lesson, we shall emphasize this truth. Some fear is very good and normal, but we will limit this study to the kinds of fear that can cause real problems in our relationship with the Lord and can hinder the labor of love to which He has called us.

Getting Acquainted

Share with someone in your class a time when, as a child, you were very frightened.

Group Discussion: What is the difference between anxiety, worry and fear?

In some ways, all three of these emotions are similar, and they frequently are experienced together. Anxiety is a deep inward reaction to uncertain circumstances. Although it does contain some fear and doubt, it is different from apprehension in that there is hopeful possibility mixed with it. Depending on upbringing and forgotten memories of danger and fear, it can become a way of life. Worry is more outward and communicative. It is a result of fear. Fear is an emotion that includes dread, apprehension and alarm, even despair. Sometimes it can even excite the individual to a desire to escape from the situation.

Group Discussion: Can you name some normal fears that actually protect us?

The Lesson

Read Matthew 13:22.

1. In this passage we find that the deceitfulness of riches can cause us to be fruitless. What else

can hinder our fruitfulness?_____

Luke brings out the fact that pleasures, riches and worry will prevent spiritual maturity. Satan and his demons are doing a thriving business today by getting God's children so taken up with their own problems that they are paralyzed in their service to the Lord and to others.

Adam and Eve became afraid and ran from what they feared.

Satan's temptation to Eve was that a fruit would make her wise and she would become like God. In essence, then, she and Adam were replacing God as the center of their life, with themselves. They could be like God!

Read Genesis 3:4-6,8-10.

2. What was Adam's answer to the Lord when God called to them in the garden?_____

_____

Whenever man has replaced his trust in the Lord with total dependence upon himself, fear takes control. Today, materialism prevails as man's god. Man has become his own god, and, while this may give him false pride for a time, yet eventually great fear, worry and anxiety will overtake him.

Read Luke 21:25,26.

3. How will the circumstances of the end times affect mankind?_____

_____

Read Revelation 6:15-17.

4. What kind of men will run and hide themselves on the day of God's wrath?_____

_____

It will not be just those kind of men who are considered timid and weak.

The world has adopted materialism and humanism as a way of life, and as the only gods to rely on. Therefore, they have plenty to fear. We see things coming upon us that are causing men's hearts to fail. An all-out nuclear war seems imminent. Drug use, immorality in many different forms, crime, suicide and rape are on the rise. People have reason to fear when they have nothing stronger than themselves to lean on!

Personal Questions: What kind of a foundation do you have to rely upon when you are tempted to fear? Is your Christian faith a practicing faith? Let's be careful lest we just play or pretend to be "Christian." What do you see when you look inside of yourself?

We must face our fears.

I had a deep fear of flying. I ran away from this fear by avoiding any opportunity to fly. The time came when I could no longer run. I had to face the situation. I could only do this with JESUS!

Read Psalm 46:1-3,5-7,10,11.

5. What practical reason do we as Christians have for not fearing?_____

_____

We need not fear "though the earth should change." (I had to learn this in order to be released from my fear of flying.)

6. What does verse 7 tell us about God?_____

_____

Group Discussion: What are some ways that we can face our fears?

Group Discussion: Name some of the fears that people have.

Christians are maturing into a Christ-centered experience.

We made the decision for Christ's lordship when we truly repented from going our own way. Yet, most of us still are self-centered to some degree, depending on our growth. In order to have good mental health and fearlessness, we need to know exactly where we stand with the Lord.

Read 2 Timothy 1:7; Matthew 16:18.

7. The spirit that God has given us consists of power, love and discipline. What kind of a spirit

has He not given us?_____

8. If we make sure that we are built on a Rock foundation, which is Jesus, what can't prevail

against us?_____

So if God has not given us the spirit of timidity and fear, then we must admit that it comes from the very gates of hell. This cannot prevail against us.

Read Matthew 7:24,25.

9. If we hear God's Word and act upon it, what are we compared to?_____

_____

We cannot be overthrown by fear, anxiety and worry if we are in a right relationship with the Lord and maturing in it.

Read Isaiah 33:13-16; 57:19-21.

10. What is the condition of the sinners and the godless?_____

11. What are the wicked compared to?_____

12. What are we to shut our eyes from?_____

13. How is God described in Isaiah 33?_____

_____

14. What kind of a rock will be our refuge?_____

15. What does this portion tell us about our bread and water?_____

We know the Lord has promised to supply our needs; therefore, we need not fear financial insecurity, if we are in a right relationship with Him (Phil. 4:19).

Worry over money problems only causes confusion of thought, and it will prevent us from good sensible thinking. Let's lay the situation before our God and expect Him to give us wisdom as to how to obtain the work we need. He can give us wisdom and guidance. God doesn't just open a window in heaven and throw the money down, but He knows how to put ideas into our minds. There are no answers for those who wish to sidestep faith in a good solid relationship with the Lord.

Read Psalm 34:4.

16. What condition is laid down in this verse by which you can be delivered from all your fears?

_____

You cannot have a sound mind, which God has promised to give you, and be a victim of fear and anxiety at the same time. You can choose which of these you really want. You can *will* to have what God wants you to have.

Do you fear what others may say or do to you?

Read Hebrews 13:5,6; Romans 8:31.

17. What great promise do we have from Scripture that can eliminate our fear of others?_____

_____

18. Write a paragraph based on Romans 8:31. What does this scripture mean to you?

Ask the Lord to help you understand your fear of other people and their reactions to you. Deliberately place yourself in the presence of someone that you are timid with. Then, little by little, increase your communication with that person over a period of time. Thus, you put feet to your prayers and will eventually overcome your fear. Never shy away from your timidity.

An undisciplined life will bring insecurity.

An undisciplined Christian is one who is careless about obeying the Word of God.

Read Isaiah 66:4.

19. Upon what kind of people will God bring fear?_____

_____

Not only do we need to be accountable to God and His Word but also to others. In fact, accountability to God includes this. Others need to know that they can rely upon us, that we are available when needed, and that we are doing our work to the best of our ability. Many times our fear of losing our job, of losing our mate, or any other fear, comes from an undisciplined life. Sometimes we all fail, but this should be the exception rather than the rule.

Read 1 John 1:9; Hebrews 4:15,16.

20. God is not angry when we make mistakes and fail Him. All He asks us to do is_____

_____

21. Scripture tells us that we can come with confidence to the throne for forgiveness and grace

to help us discipline ourselves. Why is this so?_____

_____

_____

This will give meaning to our life, opportunity to be a blessing to others, a confidence in God's help for the future.

Read 2 Corinthians 13:5.

22. What should we test or examine?_____

_____

We must make sure of our relationships with the Lord.

23. Remember the commands in the following verses.

Isaiah 41:10a_____

_____

2 Kings 6:16_____

_____

Revelation 1:17_____

_____

Matthew 10:24-26_____

_____

Luke 12:31,32_____

_____

God's Word is a source of healing for the fear of death.

Most people suffer from the fear of death. In a sense, death is still an enemy to God's people.

Read 1 Corinthians 15:53-57.

24. When will the Christian's enemy, death, be swallowed up in victory?_____

_____

25. Who gives us the victory over the enemy?_____

Group Discussion: What has been done to the sting of death?

Group Discussion: In what ways would death still be an enemy to us?

God will give grace for the day of death.

Read Matthew 6:34; 2 Corinthians 12-9.

26. What does this passage tell us about each day?_____

27. What does the Lord promise us about His grace?_____

_____

Read 1 Peter 5:7.

28. What are we to do with all our cares and anxieties?_____

I believe according to the above scriptures that God's grace will be available for each day's needs. When we fear for the day of death before time, we only ask for trouble. I will not receive help today for what I must go through tomorrow or later. Whatever a day brings forth, it will also bring the help I need from the Lord. If we can take hold of this truth by faith, it can help us through many other areas of fear and anxiety.

While some friends were talking about death, one old lady said, "I am not looking for the undertaker, but for the uptaker." (Praise the Lord!)

It is the gateway into a far greater and more perfect life with the Lord!

Read Philippians 1:21,23.
29. Write these passages in your own words and tell what they mean to you.

Abnormal and deep fears such as phobias usually start in early childhood. Parents somehow relay to their children their own fears, and these in turn become stronger than the parents' fears. Children look to their parents for comfort, and have deep trust in them. If the parents think something is dangerous, it must be. This is the attitude of the child.

Group Discussion: What effect did your parents' fears have on you?

A strong faith in the Lord can change all this.
A good study of God's love can cast out any kind of fear, even if the fear is long-standing.
Read 1 John 4:18,19.
30. God loves us far more than any human being could love. What a thought! What is the real

power that casts out fear?_____
When we really believe that God not only loves us but is in complete control of us, we begin to feel secure. Only the Word of God brings this out. Unbelievers think of God as a strong moralist "looking down their necks," ready to punish them. Only those who have tasted of His salvation have found out the truth. He loves them and has drawn them with cords of love.
Women who have strong phobias need to stay close to Jesus and meditate on His Word.
How can we deal with strong fears?
Read 1 Corinthians 2:3.
31. What was Paul's confession?_____

_____

Ask the Lord for an understanding of your fear. You can experience that fear with the Lord's help by getting close to it and going into the fear one step at a time. The Lord will go with you. If you have a fear of high places, deliberately go somewhere where it is high and take a few steps at a time. Work at it over a period of time.

Exercise 1   Pair off with the members of your class and name the fears that plague you. If you have none, just be thankful and help the other person. If someone has difficulty with her fear, contact the teacher of your group. You may have to get help to take authority over that problem in the name of Jesus and cast it out. It is important to pray with each other concerning these needs.

Exercise 2   Praise brings a deep sense of the presence of God (Ps. 22:3). Spend a few minutes at the end of this session in real praise and thankfulness to God for deliverance from all fear and anxiety.

Continue at Home

To search yourself

1. Do I believe it is important to seek through the Word of God and prayer, a deeper faith in the Lord and His Word, to understand and get to know the doctrinal principles of a strong foundation?

2. What are areas in my life where I need to become more disciplined and faithful to the work of the Lord.

3. Can I meditate on the memory verses and learn to think only positive thoughts?

To focus
The challenging thought of this lesson is

I can use it this week

To memorize
"There is no fear in love; but perfect love casts out fear, because fear involves punishment, and the one who fears is not perfected in love. We love, because He first loved us" (1 John 4:18,19).

"For God has not given us a spirit of timidity, but of power and love and discipline" (2 Tim. 1:7).

"Do not fear, for I am with you; do not anxiously look about you, for I am your God. I will strengthen you, surely I will help you, surely I will uphold you with My righteous right hand" (Isa. 41:10).

DIARY ENTRY

DAY	TIME SPENT WITH THE LORD	SPECIAL TRUTHS THE LORD SHOWED ME
Monday		
Tuesday		
Wednesday		
Thursday		
Friday		
Saturday		

6

Blessed Are The Merciful

Starting Point

I was able to take new courage over anxious thoughts in the following way:

I am going to refuse to worry during the next week except in a designated time. I shall follow my worry with prayer and record the results.

Check	Worry time—15 Mins.	Prayer Time—10 Mins.	Result
Sunday			
Monday			
Tuesday			
Wednesday			
Thursday			
Friday			
Saturday			

This chart will help you eliminate worry entirely when you see how foolish it really is.

Getting Acquainted

Pair off in your class and relate to your partner someone you met in grade school whom you remember vividly because he/she showed love in a special way.

Group Discussion: Do you think there is a difference in the way you feel when you say, "I'm sorry," and when you say, "Forgive me?"

Group Discussion: What is the difference between just forgetting an injustice and really forgiving?

 # The Lesson

Offenses will come to all of us.

Unforgiveness can be a big part of a deep depression. In continuous anger, there is always this problem. It can be directed many times against the Lord as well as against others or even self. Since we will be offended many times, how are we going to handle it?

I carried many offenses around in my memory for years. I felt, at the time, that these people had deliberately wanted to hurt me, although this may not have been true. Since I was forced to see these people from time to time, I suffered great mental distress just before each visit. Usually, however, I would have a good time while visiting, but this problem would be there fomenting deep within me.

I do not suffer any longer because I have been able to face the reasons for their actions. They were prejudiced because of religious differences and their attitudes were their own problems and not mine. How often we take on other people's problems and make them our own by becoming upset, bitter and depressed. The sad part is that many of those who offend us are professing Christians.

Read Psalm 55:12,13; 1 Samuel 26:7-9, 11-17, 23-25.

1. David had a problem with King Saul, and yet he was very forgiving and caring. What are some

of David's words that show his concern and forgiving attitude?_____

_____

Both David and Saul had been in close fellowship with the Lord through the prophet Samuel. They were equals even though King Saul was viewed by many people at that time as David's enemy.

Read John 13:18.

This scripture refers to Judas Iscariot who betrayed Jesus.

2. What kind of a relationship did Jesus have with Judas before his betrayal?_____

_____

Group Discussion: If Judas had truly repented, would Jesus have forgiven him?

You remember that we have read the scripture where Jesus prayed, "Father, forgive them for they know not what they do." Long before people claim their pardon, if they ever do, that pardon was paid for. Jesus already had it in His heart!

Group Discussion: Do you think that we should forgive those who offend us before they ask for it? If so, in what way?

This seems to be Jesus' example. For our own mental health, we should do so. However, to receive the benefit of forgiveness, each individual must claim it, and truly repent.
Read Matthew 18:21,22.
3. How many times should we forgive one particular person who offends us?_____
Read Matthew 6:12.
4. How should we expect God to forgive us?_____
Read Ephesians 4:32; Colossians 2:13.
5. On what basis are we obligated to forgive others?_____
6. How many of our trespasses have been forgiven by the Lord?

Just our past sins_____

Only our worst sins_____

We have to pay for some of our sins_____

All our sins_____
Read Isaiah 64:6; James 2:10.
7. How does God's Word view your need for forgiveness?_____

_____

8. How guilty were we in the eyes of the Lord?_____

_____

Read 1 John 1:7.
9. If we walk in the light as He is in the light, what two beautiful promises do we have?_____

_____

The word *cleanses* pertains to a continuous cleansing of our sins. It means that Jesus' blood will continue to cleanse and take care of all our future sins through repentance and forgiveness, if we walk in His light. We, therefore, must love and forgive as God has forgiven us. As the blood continually cleanses, even so we continue to forgive others who fail us.

Exercise 1   As a group, read the parable Jesus gave in Matthew 18:23-35. For a few minutes bow your head and picture yourself as the slave who owed his master 10,000 talents. This was your relationship with the Lord, and He has forgiven you. The first step in forgiving others is to forgive yourself. If you are not sure that God has forgiven you, ask Him to do so now. If you still feel guilty, ask for some prayer with your leader after your study today. Ask the Lord to help you forgive yourself.

Personal Questions: How is your attitude toward your own guilt at this point? How do you go about facing up to your guilt? Do you try to run away by refusing to think about it?

We must rid ourselves of all guilt in an upright way.

Guilt is dangerous. Whether it is false or true guilt, it can tamper with our relationship with God. If we know that God has forgiven us, we must forgive ourselves. Guilt held in our hearts too long produces depression.

Read 1 John 3:21; Romans 14:22,23.

10. What is the condition by which we can have confidence with God?_____

_____

If we carry guilt against ourselves, we also carry unforgiveness. Under these conditions, we do not really believe that God has forgiven us.

11. Finish this statement from Romans 14:23. "Whatever is not from faith_____."

Whatever I allow myself to do or be, I must also have the confidence that the Lord is not holding that against me. This comes from a good understanding of the Word of God. I want God to be well-pleased with me at all times. This is my goal!

Group Discussion: What is the difference between false guilt and true guilt?

What does guilt actually consist of?

Guilt is the terrible feeling of conviction that a person has when she has violated something that is part of God's law. We know that governmental laws are also a part of God's commands. Sometimes, it can be a bad feeling as a result of going against social laws as well. This last feeling could be false guilt that needs to be erased from our minds.

What is false guilt?

False guilt can come from different sources, such as rigid upbringing, social mores, or customs of a race or country. It can also be the result of rejection by our peers or someone we love or admire. Actually, underlying every kind of false accusation is Satan who has been called, "The accuser of the brethren." We need to know the difference between true guilt and false guilt. This can come from a good understanding of the Word of God. The Bible shows us what God dislikes, and this should be the kind of evil we confess and forsake. The other kind should be faced and forgotten with the Lord's help.

Read Revelation 12:10; Job 1:9-11.

12. How often does Satan accuse those who belong to the Lord?_____

_____

13. It might be a good idea for you to look up the word *accuse* for its real meaning._____

_____

When one is called an *accuser,* it means that he has this particular trait in his very personality. We also know that Satan is a liar. He likes to falsely accuse us.

14. How did Satan accuse Job?_____

_____

Group Discussion: How do you know that this accusation was false?

Read Psalm 139:23,24.

15. Sometimes we have a sense of guilt without really knowing why. What can we do at a time like

that? _____

God is faithful.

   If we ask God to search us and bring to our attention anything that is wrong, He is faithful and will show us. He also wants us to know if our guilt is false or true. False guilt can destroy us as much as true guilt if it condemns us and takes away our confidence and joy.

Read Hosea 4:6.

16. What is the cause of destruction of God's people according to this passage?_____

_____

Read James 4:17.

17. How is sin defined in James?_____

_____

   When we know from God's Word that something is wrong and we disobey, that brings true guilt, and we need to face what we did and confess it. We need forgiveness in that situation. Everyone is involved with true guilt before he comes to Christ.

Read Romans 3:19; Galatians 3:24.

18. What is the importance of having true guilt in the first place?_____

_____

   False guilt from our past life may have to be faced and forgotten. Very rigid and legalistic families sometimes have a large list of dos and don'ts as a result of religion or customs. What should we do with these? Children grow up feeling guilty because they have not been able to live up to all these laws. They become depressed.

   Much of this is false guilt and we just need to put it away. We can trust the Lord to teach us to move ahead in obedience to Him. Let the love of God be the guide in our relations with others and ourselves. We can know His Word and follow His leading. Make sure that the joy of the Lord is your strength.

Forgiving others.

   When you are ready to put away your guilt and receive full pardon, then you are ready to forgive others as well. Not only will you forgive them, but you will have a forgiving spirit as a constant thing. You will become a merciful person like your heavenly Father. Keep remembering that the measuring rule for guilt is the Word of God. Throw out any guilt that has come from Satan's suggestions or the judgments of other people.

   We have already studied the scriptures that showed how Jesus has forgiven us. Our great load of sin has been rolled on Him, and we are free. No matter how much evil others do to us, it can't amount to that for which we have been forgiven. I can easily forgive others when I think of all the times I have hurt my wonderful Lord.

Group Discussion: Can you name some attitudes that keep us from forgiving others?

Group Discussion: Name some reasons why we should forgive others besides the fact that God has forgiven us.

Read Matthew 7:1-5.

19. What does Jesus tell us not to do?_____

20. What can happen to us if we judge one another?_____

Group Discussion: What kind of judgment is Matthew referring to?

I believe this judgment is referring to motives of the heart. So many times people say and do things to us that they never intended to do. We cannot see their motives, and, when we forgive, we are leaving the judgment to God. Also, if someone did want to hurt you, it is his problem. You only make it your problem when you allow it to build resentment within you. You do not have to give anyone the satisfaction of hurting you.

Let us be careful then to stay out of other people's problems, by not allowing what they do to us fester in our hearts.

Read Romans 13:8; 14:12,13.

21. What do we owe to one another?_____

22. What reason is given in Romans 14:12 for not judging one another?_____

_____

The world's way of doing things is to return evil for evil. God wants us to return good for evil.

Someone challenged Abraham Lincoln to get rid of his enemies. He answered, "I do." The question came, "How?" He said, "By making them my friends." Returning good for evil has this effect. It is Christ's command.

Read 1 Peter 4:8.

23. What kind of love should we have for others?_____

24. What will be the result of this kind of love?_____

_____

There may come a time when you do need to go to someone about what he/she did to you. A good way of doing this would be to say, "You came across to me in such a way. Did you really mean to do that, or was I misjudging you? I sincerely hope I was." When we sincerely want to make things right with one another, the Holy Spirit can help us to do so in a way that will bring healing to both.

Read 2 Corinthians 5:21; 1 Peter 2:24; Matthew 27:46.

25. Study these three passages of Scripture, and then write a paragraph on what it really cost Jesus to

forgive you. _____

_____

_____

_____

_____

Read Galatians 3:13.

26. What did Jesus actually become when He redeemed us?_____

Since it cost Jesus so much to forgive us, we know that He didn't just forget our offenses. He did not say, "Just forget it."

Someone once said that if we had the same circumstances of life as someone who had sinned, we would probably do the same thing. I'm not completely sure of that, but I know that if we would look at ourselves from God's eyes, we would be just as guilty.

Group Discussion: Can you think of some ways in which it does cost us something to forgive another who sins against us?

When we forgive, we freely bear the results of that offense. Some years ago a Christian woman's reputation was damaged by another person. Others were involved and influenced. When the offender asked for pardon, it was granted. However, because the damage was unrepayable, the forgiver had to bear the results of that offense. She did it graciously! Her forgiveness of that person was costly, but she felt it was worth it. Jesus does take care of the damage if we leave it to Him. He bore it on the cross, and we need not continue to carry the load. If we demand payment, we are not forgiving.

Read Hebrews 2:9.

27. What did Jesus taste for us and in our place?_____

Read Colossians 3:13.

28. Fill in the blanks. "Bearing with one another, and _____each other, whoever has

a _____against anyone; just as the _____ _____ _____, so also should you."

Group Discussion: When we don't forgive immediately, who is doing the most suffering?

Group Discussion: If forgiveness from God restores our fellowship with Him, what should our forgiveness of one another restore? What are some ways that we can do this?

 Exercise 2   Forgiving is an action. Think of someone who has recently offended you and write on the chart below some ways you can show your forgiveness of that person (Eph. 4:32).

Be Kind   How

Tenderhearted   How

Forgiving   How

Exercise 3   Looking at Ephesians 4:31, write down on the chart below some things you do when you allow the following characteristics to continue.

Resentfulness   I do_____

_____

_____

Anger   I do_____

_____

_____

Slander   I do_____

_____

_____

These things affect me spiritually in the following ways:

Continue at Home

To search yourself

1. Have I ever made a real commitment ahead of time to be forgiving at all times? Am I willing to do so now and trust the Lord to help me?

2. Do I understand what compassion really means? I will look up the meaning.

3. Do I practice looking for the good qualities in those that I come into contact with and remember to pray for those who have weaknesses?

To do

1. Make sure that you do not go to bed at night without asking for forgiveness if you have offended your husband or children in any way. Never let offenses pile up between you and family members.

2. Record on the following chart the times in this coming week that you offend the individual members of your family. Also record when you ask their forgiveness for those offenses. Record also those times when you offend others outside your home.

	Offense	Forgiven
Sunday		
Monday		
Tuesday		
Wednesday		
Thursday		
Friday		
Saturday		

This chart will help you to be more consciously aware of your consideration of others, and you may find yourself offending others less often. You may not have to use this chart every day. You may not have to use it at all.

To focus

The most help I have received from this lesson is

I can use it this week

To memorize

"But go and learn what this means, 'I desire compassion, and not sacrifice,' for I did not come to call the righteous, but sinners" (Matt. 9:13).

"Blessed are the merciful, for they shall receive mercy" (Matt. 5:7).

"You have heard that it was said, 'You shall love your neighbor, and hate your enemy.' But I say to you, love your enemies, and pray for those who persecute you" (Matt. 5:43,44).

DIARY ENTRY

DAY	TIME SPENT WITH THE LORD	SPECIAL TRUTHS THE LORD SHOWED ME

Monday

Tuesday

Wednesday

Thursday

Friday

Saturday

7

Steps Toward
A Good Self-Image

Starting Point

I can use what I felt was the outstanding thought of Lesson Seven in the following way:

I am still having problems in accepting myself in this particular area of my personality:

I believe I have made some progress in practicing what I have learned by

Getting Acquainted

Share with a new partner concerning a blessing or something special that the Lord has done for you the past week.

Group Discussion: What is the difference between pride and a healthy self-respect? Do you feel that self-respect is a form of pride? If so, would it be a sinful thing, or a normal, human characteristic?

The Lesson

God has not rejected anyone.

A big sin is committed by the one who rejects herself. God does not reject her; God has open arms for all.

Read 2 Peter 3:9; Revelation 22:17.

1. What does the Lord want for all His human creatures?_____

_____

2. For whom is the fountain of the water of life opened?_____

One of the reasons that rejection of self is a serious offense against God is because, if allowed to continue and grow, it can breed so many other evils.

Read 1 Samuel 15:23.

3. How does the Lord compare rebellion and insubordination?_____

_____

If we continue to reject ourself as a matter of course, it will breed evils such as rebellion against God and other associates as well. There is a tendency to become critical and harsh. The motive is to build ourself up by tearing someone else down. It is a desperate attempt, perhaps an unconscious attempt, to build up a defense against our own self-hate. This is an escape route we all need to become aware of; it doesn't help us at all.

Read Psalm 42:3-5; Hebrews 10:25.

4. When the psalmist became depressed, what did he stop

doing?_____

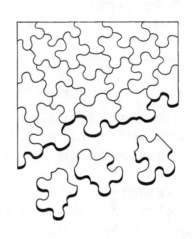

_____

A person who hates and rejects herself will also have a tendency to withdraw from other people. She is an unhappy person and becomes overly sensitive towards what others do or say. She may even find it difficult to go to church.

Group Discussion: What are some areas in which a person can reject herself?

Personal Questions: Do you enjoy mixing in with a group of God's children and look forward to the times when you can do so? Do you look forward to your Sunday morning church attendance? If not, why not?

A long history of self-rejection and withdrawal will cause a person to look for happiness elsewhere. Without realizing why she is doing it, a woman will sometimes overdress and concentrate on her appearance. She will look for happiness in material possessions. A woman who feels good about herself will want to dress well, but only so she can forget about herself and continue to attend to the Lord's business.

Read Matthew 6:31-33.

5. What is the condition given in this passage of scripture for the Lord to supply our needs?

_____

_____

6. What are all the things that will be added to us?_____

_____

Poor self-image causes self-centeredness.

In her desperate attempt to accept herself, a person will center everything that transpires around herself. She is the very center. She cannot afford to encourage others for fear that it takes even more self-respect from her.

Group Discussion: Discuss for a few moments what it really means to seek the kingdom of God first.

Group Discussion: What are some of the reasons a person who is self-centered cannot truly put the kingdom of God first in her life?

Read Philippians 2:3,4.

7. What are the three commands in this scripture?_____

_____

_____

Group Discussion: Many people who have a problem of self-rejection are so aware of their own shortcomings, they consider others as superior to themselves. What is the difference between this attitude and God's command to "regard one another as more important than himself" (Phil. 2:3)?

There is a difference.

In the first instance, they may consider others superior, but will look for opportunities to criticize or hurt them in some way. This is also an opening for jealousy and envy to breed and cause depression.

Read James 3:13-18.

8. How does this passage in *James* describe jealousy, envy or selfish ambition?_____

9. What is the final result of these evil things?_____

10. Looking at verses 17 and 18, we understand the results of "regarding one another as more

important than ourselves," as God commands us. What are those results?_____

_____

Group Discussion: Parents with low self-esteem can destroy their children's self-esteem. What are some of the ways in which they can do this? Have you ever heard this statement: "You will never amount to anything anyway"?

When parents have a poor self-image, they strive for superiority in their home. Actually, parents are not superior to their children; they are, however, more experienced. They need to give their children the benefit of their experiences.

Prestige-centered parents will cause power struggles in their children.

Children often endeavor to get their parents into a struggle for power. Our prestige takes a beating when our children defy us, and that defiance causes our self-esteem to plummet even further. We need respect from our children, not a struggle for power, or fear.

Read Philippians 2:4.

Group Discussion: In light of this passage, what should a mother's main interest be in relationship to her child?

Instead of being self-centered, a mother must become situation-centered. "What does this situation call for?" should be her thought when dealing with a child. A healthy self-estimation will help her in this respect. When we as parents can evaluate ourself in the light of God's Word, we can afford to let our children know that we make mistakes and to ask their forgiveness when we do. We can show love and concern by encouragement and proper commendation. At the same time we must make firm rules that they can understand.

Group Discussion: What are some of the interests about which a mother should be concerned regarding her children?

I like the explanation of Philippians 2:3, as given by the commentary of Jamieson, Fausset and Brown. "The direct relation of this grace is to God alone; it is the sense of dependence of the creature on the Creator as such, and it places all created beings in this respect on a level. The man 'lowly of mind' as to his spiritual life is independent of men, and free from all slavish feelings, while sensible of his continual dependence on God. Still it indirectly affects his behavior toward his fellowmen; for, conscious of his entire dependence on God for all his abilities, even as they are dependent on God for theirs, he will not pride himself on his abilities, or exalt self in his conduct toward others."

Going on further in their explanation, we read, "Instead of fixing your eyes on those points in which you excel, fix them on those in which your neighbor excels you: this is true 'humility.' The oldest manuscripts read, 'Not looking each of you (plural, Greek) on his own things (i.e., not having regard solely to them), but each of you on the things of others' also.'"

When we are born again, filled with the Spirit of God, we begin to see from the standpoint of God's Word. We begin to see ourselves and others even as the Lord sees. What a difference!

Read Galatians 6:1-3,9,10.

11. What are some of the ways that we can become situation-centered in our relations with other

Christians? _____

_____

Poor ideas about ourself will cause us to draw within ourself and not reach out to others. On the other hand, when our attitude about ourself is healthy, we can afford to be situation-centered in being aware of the needs in those around us. We can afford to become more concerned about others' needs than our own. We choose to love with God's kind of love. This means that we give of ourself in the process to our children and to others, without wanting to hurt them or ruin them with just natural or emotional love.

Read 1 John 4:7-11; John 13:34,35.

12. Agape love is commanded by Jesus; merely natural or emotional love cannot be commanded. Write a paragraph, using the material in the above passages. Show that it is a command from Jesus and that we must truly obey._____

_____

_____

_____

_____

We must start with ourselves.

Emotionally sick people are incapable of giving or receiving this agape love. If you want to be healthy, start giving this love, first to yourself, and then to others. You can love your neighbor as yourself without expecting anything in return.

Read Romans 9:1-4.

13. Paul, the apostle, had a healthy self-esteem and gave of himself to others continually. How did he feel for his fellow Israelites?_____

_____

Personal Questions: Are you resentful toward yourself for any particular reason? Will you begin to understand God's kind of love for you and accept it? Are you feeling resentful toward someone else?

I will identify my resentment in the space below:

_____

I will admit that in my flesh I cannot get rid of this resentment. I can do so by

_____

I will demonstrate God's love to that person by

_____

I will talk this over with Jesus and also with

_____

I will wait in the Lord's presence and let His love sweep over me.

We must help one another to growth and victory.

I heard a sermon sometime ago concerning the raising of Lazarus that made an impression on me and emphasized an important truth.

Read John 11:32-44.

14. Describe the appearance of Lazarus when he came out of the tomb._____

_____

15. After the mighty miracle was accomplished, what did Jesus tell the people to do?_____

_____

Lazarus was bound.

   Even though physical life had been restored to Lazarus, he could not function until he was loosed by the people around him and set free. Some Christians have thought that as soon as new life is given to us, we are automatically victorious and healed; that we are completely delivered from all our sinful bondages. This is not necessarily true. However, we now have a miraculous potential to be free.

Group Discussion: In what sense do we help and encourage new Christians in freeing them from poor self-images and their other bondages? We know that it is only the Word of God and the Holy Spirit that can cause them to grow and bring them freedom. What are some ways in which we can help?

Read 1 Thessalonians 5:22,23.

16. What is Paul's prayer for these Thessalonian Christians?_____

_____

_____

_____

_____

Only the Lord brings true healing.

   The world believes that it has an answer to the lack of self-esteem, and many of God's children fall prey to its philosophies. The world believes that we can all realize the potential that lies within us, such as self-realization, etc. It likes to tell us that we all have a divine spark; that we should recognize the god-power within us and release it. Such ideas are not the answer and, in fact, will lead us to spiritual ruination.

Read Deuteronomy 33:27-29; Psalm 32:7,8.

17. We must recognize our helplessness without God. Our self-esteem is not built on our own

resources. Who must we recognize as our refuge?_____

18. Where are the everlasting arms in relationship to us?_____
19. In verse 29 God compares His children in relation to other people. Write out this verse in

your own words. _____

_____

_____

_____

We must understand where our power for living is coming from.

   When we realize this, we see a very good balance of healthy self-acceptance begin to emerge.

We experience depression when our relationships in this world become more important to us than our surrender to the Master. Here is where new purpose and love for the Lord, for others and ourselves begins. We identify with each of these in love.

Read Philippians 4:13; Colossians 1:29.
20. Where do we get our strength to "do all things"?_____
Read Romans 8:31-39.
21. After reading this passage, write a paragraph and show from it the value and investment God

had in you when He sent His Son to save you._____

_____

_____

_____

_____

_____

I must begin to cast away the old life and attitudes.
Read Isaiah 55:8-13.

Everything must now bow to our new spiritual life. Many of us, before salvation, communicated the message to others to get away from us because we were not lovable. Many of us had parents who may have told us that we would never amount to anything, who in action and words rejected us. Many of us, as a result, grew up to pull away from our husband and other relationships.

22. What does the Lord tell us about His thoughts and ways?_____

_____

Read 2 Corinthians 10:4,5.
23. What are we to do with our old ideas, imaginations and thoughts?_____

_____

_____

In our next chapter we will be meditating on the way God sees us in Jesus. This should send us on our way rejoicing!

Exercise 1   Most of us have areas in our nature or our appearance that we regret and can do little about. Pair off with someone and confess this resentment. Pray for each other for the willingness to accept this; to be thankful as well.

Exercise 2   Divide into small groups of two or three. Think of a gift or talent God has given you and share this with each other. Give the Lord all the glory and be especially appreciative to Him.

Continue at Home

To search yourself

1. Visualize by faith what you would like to do or become in God's kingdom, and, after prayer for guidance, write this down. Pray over this each day. God will show you if this needs to be changed.

2. Check your life in matters of obedience so that you can hear from the Lord from time to time during your morning devotions.

3. For one week keep a record in the following chart of each time that you hear yourself complaining about anything.

Sunday _____

Monday _____

Tuesday _____

Wednesday_____

Thursday_____

Friday_____

Saturday_____

To focus

The outstanding thought of this lesson for me was

I can use this thought and practice this in my daily walk by

To memorize

"And let us consider how to stimulate one another to love and good deeds, not forsaking our own assembling together, as is the habit of some, but encouraging one another, and all the more, as you see the day drawing near" (Heb. 10:24,25).

"I can do all things through Him who strengthens me" (Phil 4:13).

"Brethren, I do not regard myself as having laid hold of it yet; but one thing I do: forgetting what lies behind and reaching forward to what lies ahead, I press on toward the goal for the prize of the upward call of God in Christ Jesus" (Phil. 3:13,14).

DIARY ENTRY

DAY	TIME SPENT WITH THE LORD	SPECIAL TRUTHS THE LORD SHOWED ME

Monday

Tuesday

Wednesday

Thursday

Friday

Saturday

8

Your Value In Heaven's Terms

(How do you estimate yourself?)

Starting Point

I have learned that I can show mercy as a challenging and exciting part of living in the following ways:

Ask the Lord to give you several opportunities during the following week to encourage another person who may be depressed. Keep a record on the chart below. This is your own private record.

Opportunity	Person	Result
1.		
2.		
3.		
4.		

The following paragraph is a further explanation of what I believe was accomplished.

Getting Acquainted

Try to remember, if possible, a rather humorous but embarrassing moment in your life to share with your neighbor. (Keep this on the light side.)

Group Discussion: Give some illustrations of what you think are bad self-estimations, in contrast to those that are healthy.

Group Discussion: How would you view the difference between superiority complexes and inferiority complexes?

 # The Lesson

Life begins with the New Birth.

How true is the above statement! We may know this to be true with our heads, but sometimes it takes awhile before we grasp its real significance.
Read Philippians 3:12-16.

1. When we first begin our new life with Jesus, there may be many things that we are not aware

of or haven't learned. However, what is the one thing that we must begin to do?_____

_____

When we grasp the real and full meaning of this truth, we must begin to put it into practice.

2. What are we to reach forward to?_____

When so much of our past has shaped our living, our outlooks, attitudes and practices, it will take a miracle of God's grace to cancel the effects, but He can do it.

The specters of the past rise up to haunt us from time to time, and the results can be devastating to our self-image. How can we really be totally free of them? First of all, it is important that we understand God's evaluation of us as is given to us through Scripture.
Read 2 Corinthians 5:17.

3. If you are in Jesus Christ at this moment, how does God see you?_____

4. What has happened to the things of the past?_____

Group Discussion: Can you name some ways by which we can look at ourself the way God sees us? If not, what are some reasons we do not view ourselves from His standpoint?

Read Ephesians 4:22-24; Romans 12:2.

5. So far, we have studied the position God has placed us in. What practical commands are given

in the above scriptures?_____

_____

_____

We see two things in the above study: the positional, and the practical. The way God sees us is positional. Our part is to fulfill the practical. However, the way God sees us should raise our self-evaluation.

6. It is natural to allow the past to affect our attitudes toward ourselves. However, if we are willing to obey and renew our mind, what will we be able to prove?_____

_____

Read Romans 12:3-5.

When you see the word *for,* it should be connected to the foregoing verses the same as the word *because.* You should read verses 2-5 together.

7. How are we to estimate ourself according to the Word of God?_____

_____

8. What kind of judgment are we to exercise in respect to how we evaluate ourselves?_____

9. Where will this judgment be coming from?_____

_____

Renewing our mind with the transforming power of the Holy Spirit, according to God's consideration of His children, will be the source of this judgment.

10. How are we related to one another and what illustration does Paul use?_____

_____

Read 1 Corinthians 12:18-27.

11. God has desired you to be in His body. Fill in the blanks in the following passages. "And the

_____cannot say to the _____, 'I have _____ _____ _____ _____';

or again the _____ to the _____, '_____ _____ _____ _____ _____

_____.' On the contrary, it is much truer that the members of the body which seem to be_____

_____ are _____; and _____ _____ of the body, which we deem_____

_____on these we bestow _____ _____ _____.''

You are very much desired and needed.

Meditating on the above statement and believing what God has said can be the springboard that raises your self-esteem to its proper level. It is important to wait on the Lord for your proper functioning in the Body of Christ, in order to have the satisfaction of serving Him. Every human being has an innate desire to serve not only God, but each other. When this is lacking, it is not surprising to find guilt, condemnation and depression with low self-esteem.

Personal Question: How do you feel about your own personal self-worth at this time?

12. Rate yourself by answering the following questions.

Do I have poor self-esteem?_____Reason?_____

_____

Have I given it much thought?_____Reason?_____

_____

Do I think of myself as a normal Christian?_____Reason?_____

_____

Do I feel good about myself?_____Reason?_____

_____

God has marvelous expectations for His human creatures.

Each human soul that is born into this world was created to fit into those expectations with a specific purpose. God does not enjoy seeing any soul destroyed and unable to fulfill those expectations.

Read Ezekiel 33:11.

13. Fill in the following blank spaces: "As I live! declares the Lord God, I _____ _____

_____ _____ _____ _____ _____ _____ _____."

Read Ezekiel 18:4.

14. What does the Bible declare concerning the ownership of every soul?_____

_____

Jesus is the only one who can give life to individual souls; not only the spiritual life, but physical life. If Jesus gave you physical life, then you can be sure that He is vitally interested in you and esteems you very highly.

Read Psalm 36:9; Jeremiah 2:13.

15. Where is the fountain of life located?_____

Read Genesis 1:27,28; Psalm 8:3-9.

16. Even King David, who wrote the above psalm, was amazed at God's high purpose for mankind. What question did he ask the Lord in verse 4?_____

_____

You will notice in the passage in Genesis that both Adam and Eve were included in God's great purpose. You may have a low self-image at this point, but you can choose to look at yourself as God sees you from this moment on, as you meditate on this psalm.

17. What does the Lord want to crown you with?_____

18. What has the Lord put under your feet?_____

There is not much hope for anyone who chooses to think of herself as the world thinks because the natural world has nothing to offer her, at least, nothing with eternity's values in view.

Jesus has restored and is restoring all that our first parents lost.
Read Romans 5:8-11; 1 Thessalonians 5:23.

19. In what kind of condition were we when Jesus Christ loved us and died for us?_____

_____

20. In what condition does the Lord want us to be in at the coming of our Lord Jesus Christ?

_____

Group Discussion: In the light of the study so far, how can children who are adopted recover their self-esteem if they have been hurt by parents who gave them up?

Group Discussion: How can children who were the products of rape or illegitimacy have a good self-image? Many Christians grow up and still suffer from poor self-esteem as a result of such circumstances.

Although God is not pleased with some of the ways by which children are conceived, He does lay claim to each soul that is given physical life ("All souls are mine"). In John 1:9 we read this truth concerning Jesus Christ. "There was the true light which...enlightens every man." A person can turn from the light, but God's love for that soul knows no limit. It is a wonderful opportunity to be first of all born and then come to know the Savior through rebirth!

So-called "unwanted" children are precious to the Lord, and they are loved by the GREATEST BEING of all! We are esteemed highly by Him!

Read Romans 8:28-39.

21. What is the precious promise given to us in verse 28?_____

_____

_____

_____

22. As trusting children, what can we be convinced of?_____

_____

There is a practical side.

So far, we have studied mostly the position that God has placed us in; a place where old things have passed away, and all things are become new; a place where we are kept in the love of God through faith; a place where we were wanted even while we were yet in sin. Yet, we must face the fact of the practical responsibility of each of us; that is, to "put on the new man."

Exercise 1   Choose a partner. Then you and your partner should bow your head and ask the Lord for wisdom. Then tell your partner one positive quality that you see in her or sense about her. Once more, bow your head and pray for your partner, that God would assure her and bless her ministry.

Exercise 2   Change partners and tell each other one or two qualities that you like in yourself. Be honest and fair with yourself. Once more, pray for each other for real victory in the area of self-esteem. This is not a mutual-admiration type of thing, but an exercise by which you can honestly see what the Lord has done for you. Give Him all the glory!

Check back to what you have written on page 70 now that you have completed this lesson to see if you have changed your attitude.

Continue at Home

To search yourself

1. Spend some of your prayer time each day of this coming week just thanking the Lord for making you worthy through His blood. Thank Him for making you one of His royal children.

2. Read 1 Corinthians 13, and place yourself as the object of love in verses 4 and 7. Are you patient with yourself, kind to yourself? Do you bear with yourself, believe in yourself? Do you put up with yourself? Do you have hope for yourself? If you do, then it is true that you love yourself, and you can learn to love your neighbor. In no way does this mean that you should compromise and excuse yourself for wrong doing.

3. Look for scriptures that show Jesus as having a good self-esteem. Write a paragraph concerning it and bring it to the class for discussion in your next lesson.

To focus

The most outstanding thought of this past lesson is

I can use it this week:

To memorize

"For Thou didst form my inward parts; Thou didst weave me in my mother's womb. I will give thanks to Thee, for I am fearfully and wonderfully made. Wonderful are Thy works, and my soul knows it very well" (Ps. 139:13,14).

"Thine eyes have seen my unformed substance; and in Thy Book they were all written, the days that were ordained for me, when as yet there was not one of them. How precious also are Thy thoughts to me, O God!' (Ps. 139:16,17).

Your Value in Heaven's Terms
(How do you estimate yourself?)

73

Diary Entry

Continue to record your time for devotion, and what the Lord shows you.

DIARY ENTRY

DAY	TIME SPENT WITH THE LORD	SPECIAL TRUTHS THE LORD SHOWED ME
Monday		
Tuesday		
Wednesday		
Thursday		
Friday		
Saturday		

9

Realization of Purposeful Living

Starting Point

I have learned from Lesson 8 that I have life because God wanted me to have life. I did not become that life simply because two people came together. God gave that life because He had a purpose for me. In order to fulfill that purpose, I will continue to remember His evaluation of my soul in the following way:

A good suggestion for the following week is to read Psalm 139 each morning. Read it prayerfully, asking the Lord to give you a special revelation of its truth for each day. Record that revelation on the following chart.

Sunday _____

Monday _____

Tuesday _____

Wednesday_____

Thursday_____

Friday_____

Saturday_____

Wait on the Lord for that revelation. The Word of God is so inspired that God can give you these revelations as you wait on Him.

Getting Acquainted

Do you recall an incident in which someone made you feel important by a simple remark they made to you? Share this with one of your group members.

Group Discussion: We have spent two lessons on the need for a good self-image. If we truly believe the evaluation that God has of us which resulted in the terrible sacrifice and price He paid for our redemption, then we are ready to realize purposeful living. What are some very simple ways that we can move ahead in this regard?

 # The Lesson

Ministry begins with knowing who you are.

One of the main purposes of the four Gospels is to show us Christ's life as our example and as one we can identify with. Yet, at the same time, we need to remember that He was not only a man. He was God! It is important that we know who He was, if we are to know who we are. *Read Matthew 16:13-19.*

1. Even as there are people today who do not know who Jesus is, there were people in His day who

did not know. What were some of the ideas that people had then?_____

_____

2. What was Peter's answer?_____

3. Where did Peter get this revelation?_____

The first heads of our race, Adam and Eve, failed to become examples for us to follow. Through them we only fail in every way. Through them we inherit condemnation, guilt, destruction and death. Through them we find ourselves in confusion, frustration, conflict and total despair!

Jesus is the only one who can give us the answer to our personal life. To realize who we are, we must study the life and ministry of Jesus, the new Head of our race. We need to recognize our completeness in Him. He is called "the last Adam" in 1 Corinthians 15:45. He accomplished for us what the first Adam failed to accomplish, and much more!

Read 1 Corinthians 15:3-5; 47-49.

4. Unless we know God's purpose for Jesus' life, we will not know the true purpose and ministry

for our life. Write out in your own words the truth found in the first three verses._____

_____

_____

_____

5. What is the comparison between Adam and Jesus?_____

_____

   Listen to the way *The Living Bible* reads: "Adam was made from the dust of the earth, but Christ came from heaven above. Every human being has a body just like Adam's, made from dust, but all who become Christ's will have the same kind of body as His—a body from heaven. Just as each of us now has a body like Adam's, so we shall some day have a body like Christ's."

   If we are going to be like Jesus in our final state, it also means that we can begin to become like Him in our ministry and character, here and now! As part of this lesson, let us go back to a very well-known Scripture.

Read Matthew 20:25-28.

6. Are the following statements true or false?

a. Jesus' main purpose for coming to earth was to be served by us._____

b. We must rule over others in order to be great._____

c. Jesus came not to be served but to serve._____

d. Gentiles rule over others and so should we._____

e. We should not expect others to serve us, but rather serve them._____

Jesus came to serve us.

   When we know this fact, and we know what a beautiful relationship we have with Jesus, we can afford to cease our self-centered ways and become genuinely concerned about others. Jesus knew that He and the Father were ONE. He was enjoying a living and vital relationship with Him every moment of His ministry. He found sheer joy in serving.

   I remember that as a young girl I felt left out many times when with my friends and companions. The fact that Jesus came "not to be ministered unto, but to minister," was made very real to me. I determined to use this scripture as a good rule for my life. It has saved me from many heartaches, even though at times I failed to appropriate it. The new human Head of our race fulfilled God's purpose for Him, and I can fulfill meaningful service as well.

Read John 14:11-15.

7. How close was Jesus to His Father?_____

8. What does Jesus promise us in this passage of scripture?_____

We will find joy in serving.

   When we suffer depression and loneliness as a result of others' lack of caring, we can overcome this by doing exactly what they are *not* doing—caring. I have found this true. The works of Jesus were of topmost quality. Miracles are important, and He has given us power to do these. However, some of these "greater works" could refer to the power of transforming lives by just extending the love of Jesus to those about us. The power of God's love is limitless and far-reaching.

We can be fulfilled as a child of God.

If you are committed to Jesus and filled with His Holy Spirit, then you can manifest the love of God to others. We have studied a great deal on how to have fellowship with God and how God evaluates each one of us. By now we are beginning to have the right kind of self-worth and can minister to others.

Read Mark 12:29-31.

The Word of God is so simple that if we obey the above commands, we will be obeying all of God's commands and finding purpose for our lives.

9. Interpret the above passages in your own words._____

_____

_____

_____

Read Philippians 4:13; Matthew 19:26.

10. How do these verses relate to the scriptures in Mark 12?_____

_____

_____

Group Discussion: Have you been saying that you *can't* love some people? What are some of the *can'ts* you have been saying about loving some people, about doing what God wants you to do, about going where God wants you to go?

Personal Questions: Are you saying that there are some family members that you *cannot* communicate with? Are you saying, "I *can't* find God's purpose for my life."

Change your can'ts to won'ts.

Most good counselors try to discourage their counselees from using the words "I can't." Going back to the Group Discussion above, trying using the words "I won't" in those same statements you have been making. I can understand why unsaved people would say that they "can't," because without the help of the Lord they are incapacitated. This is not true with us: we have much power to work with.

Read 1 Corinthians 10:13.

11. What does God promise us when we are tempted to give in to weakness?_____

_____

_____

If we have a tendency to be depressed easily, it may be because we are either ignorant of what the Lord is telling us in His Word, or we are choosing not to live by His commands.

Since we know that Jesus came and fulfilled God's purpose for His life, so we, too, can be fulfilled as human beings. We can know why we are here, and where we are going.

Read Colossians 3:23,24; 1 Corinthians 10:31.

12. These passages show us how we can begin to overcome any depression. What can be the determining factor, as given here?_____

Group Discussion: What are some of the prayer requests we should include each morning during our meditation that will help us to be dedicated to the purpose of glorifying the Lord Jesus?

Pray for direction each day.
Read John 5:19-21; John 16:13.
   We need to continually view our Head, our Leader, and to follow His example.

13. How did Jesus fulfill the Father's purposes while here on earth?_____

_____

14. How are we going to get our guidance and understanding?_____
   We will be a joyful people only if we have purpose in our life.
Read Colossians 2:9,10.
15. If we are in Christ, and Christ is in us, what will be the outcome?_____

   As God's children, we are in full ministry if we are in Christ. We may be a full-time mother and wife, but, if we are in Christ, our ministry is a fulfilling one. Wherever God puts us, we can be directed by the Holy Spirit and mightily used of God. We may not be in the limelight as far as people are concerned, but God knows and keeps the books for future reference.

   It is only when a life is meaningless that people feel like committing suicide. You may be selling real estate. That is just a means to an end. Your real purpose is showing Jesus Christ as Lord and letting your life witness to the fact. There is no monotony in Jesus. Wherever you are, you have the solution to people's problems, in Jesus. We are all full-time ministers wherever God has put us.
Read Proverbs 3:5,6.
16. What conditions do we have to meet if God is going to direct our path?_____

_____

_____

   If we know that we have fulfilled the conditions, then we can be sure He is directing us. We will see miraculous events transpire in our life and the lives of those we encounter for Jesus.
Read Hebrews 10:25; 13:17.
17. What responsibility do we have to other Christians in the assembly?_____

18. What opportunity do we have for submission?_____

19. What will our leaders do for us?_____

Group Discussion: Who are the leaders of the church?

Group Discussion: If you are having a hard time submitting to others, think of how Jesus Christ submitted to His heavenly Father. Think of ways that the Father submits to His Son. Think of ways that the Holy Spirit submits to Jesus.

Read Isaiah 57:15.

20. What does God promise for those who are truly humble and contrite?_____

Exercise 1   As a group decide on three practical ways in which each one present can be a help to one person each week of her life.

Group Discussion: Can you think of ways in which these three ways can avert depression in those who participate?

Exercise 2   Take time out as a group to pray and ask the Lord to guide you to those He would have you minister to each week.

Continue at Home

To search yourself

1. How can I have a better relationship with my husband, children, parents, or someone else I am close to? Do I show them love even when they are unlovely?

2. How might I better seek the Lord's guidance for my daily tasks?

3. Am I taking time out to develop my talents or hobbies?

4. (If married) Is my sex life what it ought to be with my husband? (He should be more important than even my children.)

5. In what ways am I being careless about my physical health? Perhaps I need to take more time for exercising and watching my diet.

To do

1. Read all the scriptures you can find on the importance of a local assembly.

2. If you are not sure that you are where God wants you to be, spend much time in prayer and and waiting on God until you know.

To focus

The most important impression I have received from this lesson is

The Lord wants me to practice this for

To memorize

"For thus says the high and exalted One Who lives forever, whose name is Holy. 'I dwell on a high and holy place, and also with the contrite and lowly of spirit in order to revive the spirit of the lowly and to revive the heart of the contrite'" (Isa. 57:15.).

"Whether, then, you eat or drink or whatever you do, do all to the glory of God" (1 Cor. 10:31).

"Trust in the Lord with all your heart, and do not lean on your own understanding. In all your ways acknowledge Him, and He will make your paths straight" (Prov. 3:5,6).

Diary Entry

Continue recording your thoughts and reactions on your Diary Page.

DIARY ENTRY

DAY	TIME SPENT WITH THE LORD	SPECIAL TRUTHS THE LORD SHOWED ME

Monday

Tuesday

Wednesday

Thursday

Friday

Saturday

10

Some Important Reminders

Starting Point

Because in Lesson Nine we have studied that Jesus is our example, I can now move ahead in obedience by

Throughout this study, and especially up through Lesson Eight, we considered the problems that can trigger depression. These, of course, stem from our reactions to various losses we face from time to time. On the following chart, check any problem listed which you may have had and fill in the spaces for causes and results. If you have had a problem that isn't listed, you can place it beside the others and proceed to fill in the cause and result. By this time, the Holy Spirit may have thrown some light on your own needs, and you can more readily understand and define them.

PROBLEMS   **CAUSES**   **RESULTS**

Anger _____

_____

Guilt _____

_____

Depression _____

_____

PROBLEMS	CAUSES	RESULTS

Worry _____

_____

Loneliness _____

_____

Getting Acquainted

Some of you may have set some new goals for yourselves as a result of this study. Take a few minutes to relate these to the person on your right.

Group Discussion: Most of the problems that we have are emotional and reactionary. How important are feelings in the life of one who is endeavoring to serve the Lord?

"If it feels good, do it"?

"I don't feel like going anywhere today!" "I can't!" "I just don't feel good about it." Feelings constitute about a third of our makeup and, therefore, are vital and serve a very important role. That's the way God intended it to be. However, feelings need to be stabilized, and we must never allow feelings to be our guide in life.

This is where the Word of God comes into the picture; and so we learn to discipline and obey what we know from the Word. If we obey what we know, rather than what we feel, we are on the way to spiritual health and a positive outlook.

The Lesson

Our God is all-knowing.

Amid the uncertainties of the kind of world we live in, where can we turn for help? I remember a part of a poem I heard one of my professors in school repeat: "Truth forever on the scaffold; Wrong forever on the throne—Yet that scaffold sways the future, and, behind the dim unknown, Standeth God within the shadow, keeping watch above His own." (James Russell Lowell).
Read Hebrews 4:12.

1. God's Word is described here as sharper than a two-edged sword. What does this sword pierce

and divide besides joints and marrow?_____

It can make a difference between what we interpret as soul, and what we interpret as spirit.

Many scriptures show us that the soul includes man's emotions. David, the psalmist, wrote, "Why are you in despair, oh my soul? and why have you become disturbed within me?" It seems as if David's spirit talked to his soul and he encouraged himself in the Lord.

Then we see from 1 Corinthians 2:11,12 that man's spirit is the part of man that can know things. When we have received God's Holy Spirit, He begins to teach us the important knowledge from God's Word, and we learn to establish our "goings" by what we *know*. Man's heart is his spirit.

Read Psalm 57:7.

2. What does David tell us about his heart?_____

_____

David continued to encourage himself with the Word of God and by trusting in that Word. When his feelings got the best of him, he took control. God wants us to allow our spirit to rule over our soul (emotions) through the power and guidance of the Holy Spirit. He works through the Word. The Spirit and the Word go together.

Read Colossians 1:9,10.

3. What was Paul's important prayer for these Colossian Christians?_____

_____

_____

_____

_____

_____

_____

Let's fill our spirit with the knowledge of the Word of God. Let's discipline ourselves and obey the passage in Hebrews 4:11,12. The Word of God shows us the difference between soul and spirit, and it is alive and active as well.

Some of us are not too thrilled with the word *discipline,* but there is no other way to a spiritually healthy and joyful life in the Lord.

Personal Questions: It might be well to stop right here and ask yourself if this is an area where you are experiencing difficulty and self-condemnation. Ask the Lord to give you the willingness to obey and move ahead into His Word with your whole being. Determine to discipline yourself.

God is all-knowing.

We must realize, then, that God knew us before we were born. Therefore, we also need to learn to *know* God in our spirit, and act accordingly. Feelings must not have the upper hand!

The problems listed on the chart at the beginning of this lesson belong in the category of emotions and feelings. They are difficulties in our emotions that most of us experience, but they do not become problems unless we are defeated by them and give them the upper hand.

Group Discussion: What are some of the things we can look for when we are tempted to uncontrolled anger?

A Christian psychiatrist once told a group of ministers' wives that wherever there is uncontrolled anger, the underlying cause is fear of some kind of loss. Some of the things we can look for in our heart is this fear, as well as a tendency to shift the blame from ourselves to others.

Group Discussion: What are some of the results of uncontrolled anger? If the tendency to hold grudges becomes a result, what can this do to our physical health? What can this do to others? What can it do to our relationship with the Lord?

Read Ephesians 4:26-32; Matthew 18:15-20; 5:23-25; Philippians 4:8.
4. On the blank lines below, fill in the parts of the above scriptures that show us that we need to

Seek forgiveness and be ready to forgive:_____

_____

Release our anger in a scriptural manner:_____

_____

_____

_____

Take care of bad relationships quickly:_____

_____

Retrain our mind toward positive thoughts:_____

_____

_____

_____

_____

_____

Underlying habits must be corrected. In most of the personal weaknesses that have caused problems in our life, there are underlying habits that keep recurring; habits that we may not be totally aware of and, therefore, cannot seem to overcome. However, if we are willing to take a good look at the Word of God with the sincere desire for the Holy Spirit to take over, there is help. There is power! It takes confidence in the Word of God.

Personal Question: If you continue to have the same difficulties with your temper or guilt, it might be a good suggestion to make a record for a week of the particular instances that bring on that guilt.

Sunday _____

Monday _____

Tuesday _____

Wednesday _____

Thursday _____

Friday _____

Saturday _____

Be sincere about keeping this record.

Read 1 Corinthians 6:9-11; 1 John 2:15-17.

5. After reading through the above passages, write down the list of evils given here._____

_____

_____

_____

6. After reading the second passage above, ask the Holy Spirit for insight to answer the following questions. Name some of the things that constitute the three categories: lust of the flesh, lust of the

eye, pride of life._____

_____

_____

Exercise 1   If you have a guilt problem, it may be good to ask for prayer from the other members at this time. You need not mention the guilt, since it may be very private. You may need wisdom as to how you might make restitution and seek forgiveness. Make sure your guilt is an honest one.

If you are still having a problem with depression, even after you feel that your guilt has been taken care of, it may be a good idea to get help from a private counselor. Make sure the counselor is well-informed about God's Word.

Every individual has been given a conscience by our Creator, but conscience by itself cannot be our guide.

Group Discussion: How would you define *conscience?*

God has given human beings this ability.
Read Romans 2:14-16.

7. Where is God's moral law written?_____

Conscience is the ability that God has given us to evaluate ourself according to that moral law, but then it only tells when we are guilty. Thus it produces warning signals that all is not right with our Creator. If we ignore this for any length of time, our conscience can become calloused and fail in its God-given purpose.

In order to have a good conscience toward God, we need to be more and more informed by the Word of God. We need to face guilt and know how to get rid of it.

Read Acts 24:16; 1 Timothy 1:5.

8. What was Paul endeavoring to maintain?_____

9. What was the goal of his instruction to Timothy?_____

_____

Jesus never sinned, and He gives, as a free gift, His perfect righteousness to those who accept Him. Only those who do, have the beautiful right to be forgiven when they fail, while going on to more and more victory!

Read Ephesians 2:8,9; Titus 3:5.

10. Write out in your own words the above scriptures._____

_____

_____

_____

Much worry is caused by guilt.

When once we are free from guilt, we can go on to obey the Lord in the following scriptures.

Read 1 Peter 5:7; Matthew 6:34; Philippians 4:6-8.

11. In this lesson, we are reviewing some of the main causes of depression and the answers from Scripture as well. Read the above passages and write them out in the following lines.

1 Peter 5:7_____

Matthew 6:34_____

Philippians 4:6,7 _____

_____

Philippians 4:8 _____

_____

The only way that our conscience will be free from guilt and worry is for us to renew our mind. One of our biggest problems is our negative thinking. Let's put that away by the renewal of our mind.

Read Romans 12:2; Ephesians 4:22-24; Colossians 3:9-11.
12. Fill in the blanks below.

"And do not be conformed to this world, but be transformed by _____ _____

_____ _____ _____ _____ _____ _____ _____ _____ _____

_____ _____ _____ _____, that which is good and acceptable and perfect" (Rom.
12:2).
"That, in reference to your former manner of life, you lay aside the old self, which is being cor-

rupted in accordance with the lusts of deceit, and that _____ _____ _____

_____ _____ _____ _____ _____ _____ and put on the new self" (Eph.
4:22,23).
"Do not lie to one another, since you laid aside the old self with its evil practices, and have put

on the new self_____ _____ _____ _____ _____ _____ _____

_____according to the image of the One who created him" (Col. 3:9,10).

  We have the responsibility to renew our mind.

Group Discussion: What are some good ways that we can do this?

Reactions to loneliness can cause depression.
  Every person, if he lives long enough, will experience loneliness, some more than others.

Personal Question: Have you ever noticed what actually causes those times of loneliness in
your life? Sometimes we are afraid to confront these reasons because they may reveal weaknesses
in us.
It is not a sin to be lonely.
  Loneliness is a normal reaction to the loss of a loved one, especially a parent, child, husband
or wife. We must, however, resolve this in time. It can be overcome.
Read Philippians 4:13.
13. How can we overcome loneliness?_____

_____

Have a regular time with the Lord in prayer.
Read Isaiah 40:31.
14. We not only find fellowship with the Lord in this way, but we gain something else. What is it?

_____

Be concerned for today only.
15. Find your own scripture that shows you that this is important.

_____

_____

Minister to others in various ways.
Read again Matthew 20:28.

16. What attitude of Jesus can we take for ourself here?_____

_____

Accept other people just as they are, and not "the way they should be."
Read Romans 5:8.

17. What was our condition when Christ loved and died for us?_____

 We can have understanding of the faults of others even if we cannot understand them.

Be forgiving even if it isn't asked for.

Read Luke 23:34.

18. What was Christ willing to do even while the people were hurting Him?_____

 Find someone to share your love with and also your burdens.

Practice communication with family and friends.

 Don't wait for others to take the first step. You may have to read some good literature on how to communicate in an interesting way, but it will be worth it.

Read 2 Timothy 4:9-13.

19. According to the above passages, how did Paul handle his prison loneliness?_____

_____

20. How did he attempt to get company for himself?_____

_____

21. How was he providing for his own spiritual encouragement?_____

22. How did Paul admit his loneliness?_____

_____

 I remember a young girl who came to me in one of our prayer meetings and admitted she was very lonely. She needed friends. It was good that she faced her loneliness and came for help. After praying with her, I asked her to go back a few seats to another girl and make her acquaintance. (I happened to know that this other girl was lonely also.) I asked her to encourage this girl and pray with her. She did! This was the beginning of a life of active service, and today she is in full-time ministry. The scripture I gave her was one that I have referred to in this study more than once. Jesus "did not come to be served, but to serve" (Matt. 20:28).

She was not to be concerned whether others served her, but rather how she could serve others. What a difference this has made in my own life!

Read Hebrews 13:5,6.

23. What reasons do we have that show us why we can afford to minister to others in

love? _____

Read John 10:27-30.

24. What kind of security has Jesus promised us?_____

_____

   I sincerely pray that this Workshop has been of help to you in finding your way into a fruitful and joyful Christian experience. It certainly is not a complete answer to all the problem areas that we face from time to time, but it can be a beginning.

> **Exercise 2**   As a group, share with each other some of your experiences with loneliness.

> **Exercise 3**   Looking at those same experiences, share some of the ways that you were helped, or could be helped if you are still lonely.

 # Continue at Home

To search yourself

   1. Ask yourself if there is some area in your life where you are not obeying the Lord. Then in your time of devotion ask the Holy Spirit to throw light on any area that is weak, and where you need more spiritual strength. Be ready to face anything He may show you and be prepared to discipline yourself.

   2. If you have been depressed, make sure that you are taking care of any guilt in the scriptural way, and begin to assume normal responsibilities. Do this whether you feel like it or not.

   3. Practice living with the problems of just one day at a time, trusting the Lord for your tomorrows. If you have a tendency to worry, try reminding yourself of this each day for one week.

To do

   1. Make a list of character traits you feel you need to change, and spend some time each day asking the Lord for His help in doing so.

   2. Keep a record for a week of each time you make a negative statement about yourself or someone else and determine, with the Lord's help, to change.

To focus

The three most important thoughts of this last lesson are

Evidently, the Lord wants me to practice these things by

To memorize

"Be anxious for nothing, but in everything by prayer and supplication with thanksgiving let your requests be made known to God. And the peace of God, which surpasses all comprehension, shall guard your hearts and your minds in Christ Jesus" (Phil. 4:6,7).

"My heart is steadfast, O God, my heart is steadfast; I will sing, yes, I will sing praises" (Ps. 57:7).

"My lips will shout for joy when I sing praises to Thee; and my soul, which Thou hast redeemed. My tongue also will utter Thy righteousness all day long; for they are ashamed, for they are humiliated who seek my hurt" (Ps. 71:23,24).

Diary Entry

Continue recording your thoughts and reactions on your Diary Page.

DIARY ENTRY

DAY	TIME SPENT WITH THE LORD	SPECIAL TRUTHS THE LORD SHOWED ME
Monday		
Tuesday		
Wednesday		
Thursday		
Friday		
Saturday		

Notes

Notes